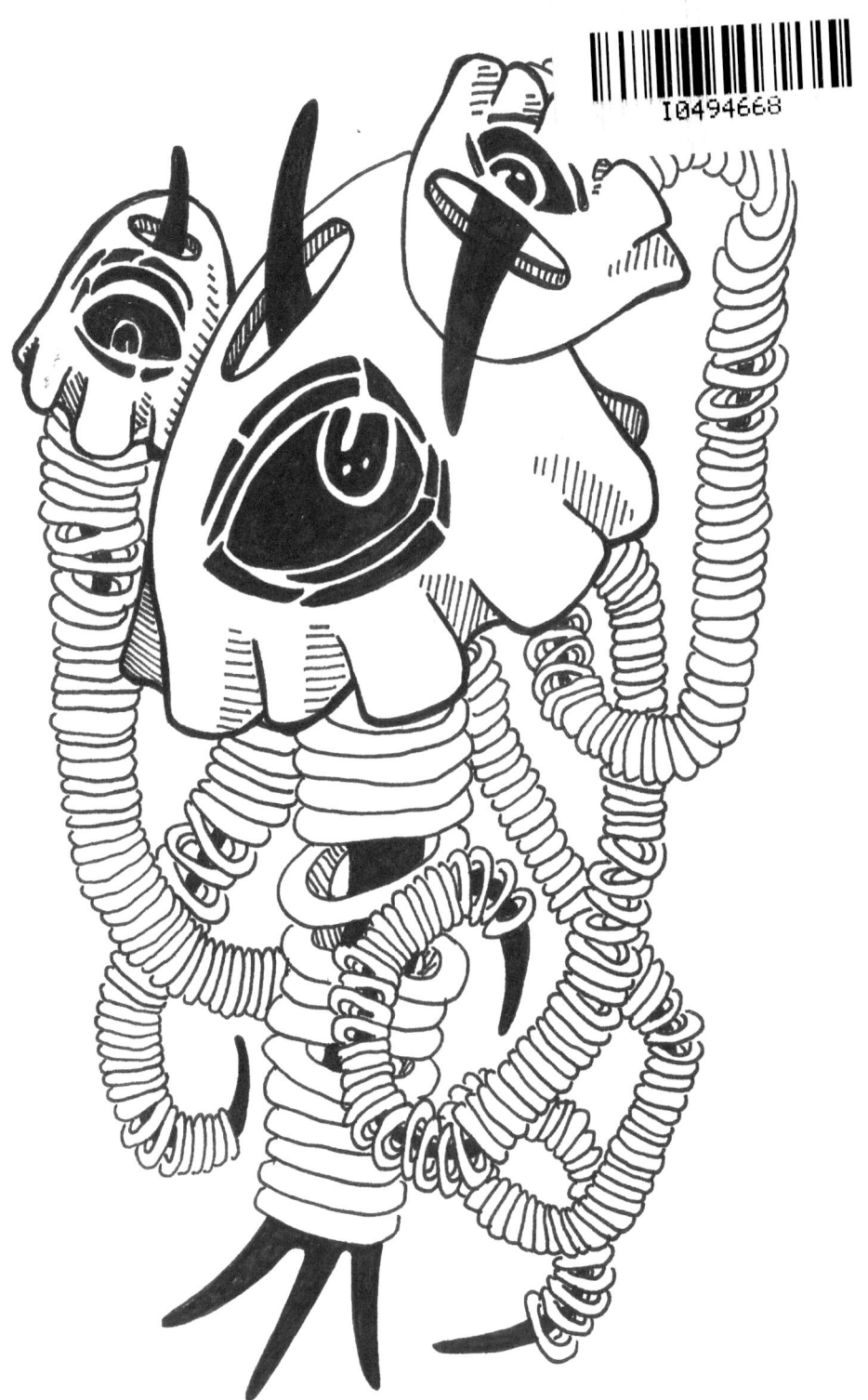

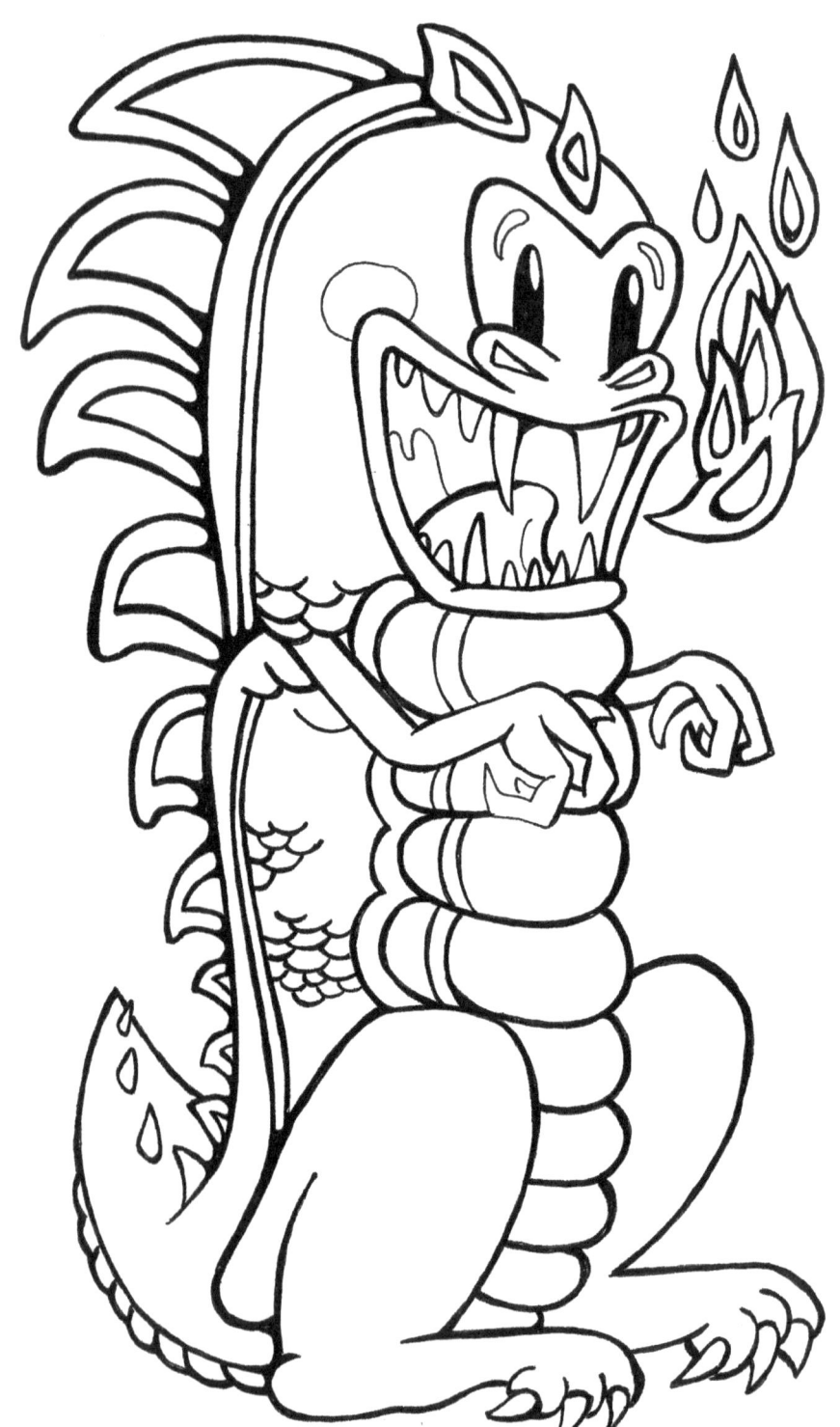

A CRAZY COMPILATION OF

COLORFUL CREATURES

WRITTEN AND ILLUSTRATED BY BOZ SCHURR

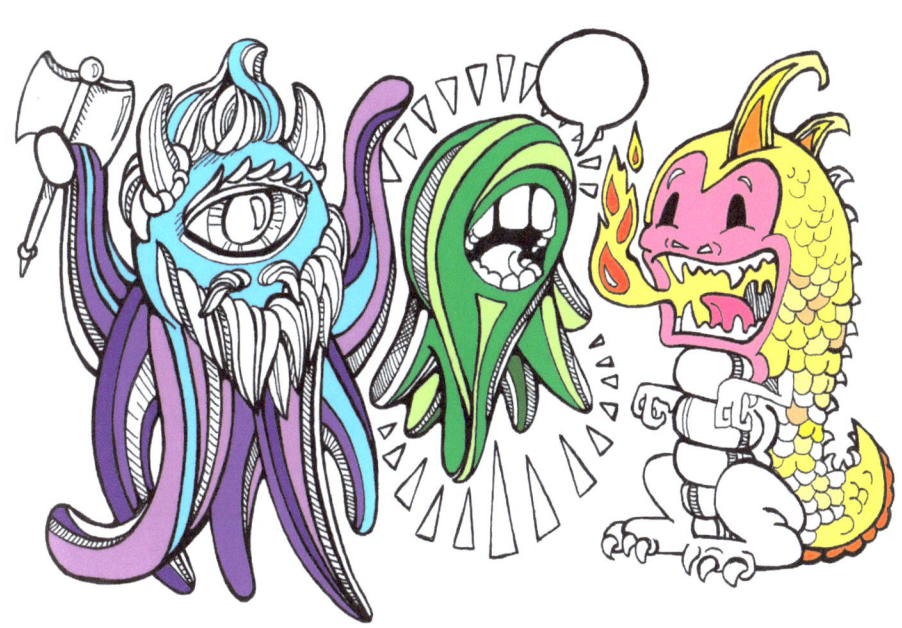

A ONE-OF-A-KIND COLORING BOOK WITH MESSY MONSTERS, DYNAMIC DINOSAURS AND CRAZY CREATIONS! PERFECT COLORING FUN FOR EVERYONE!

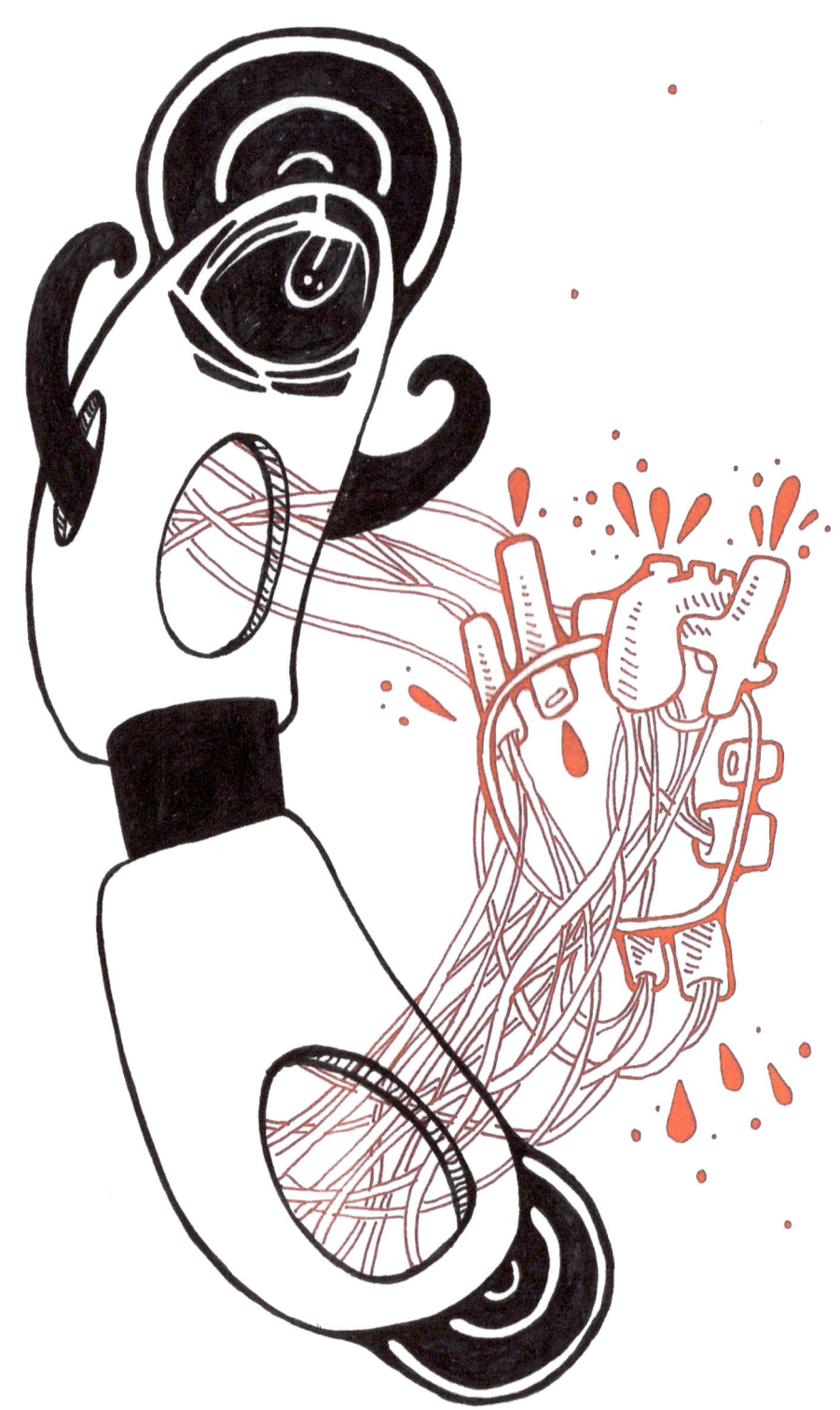

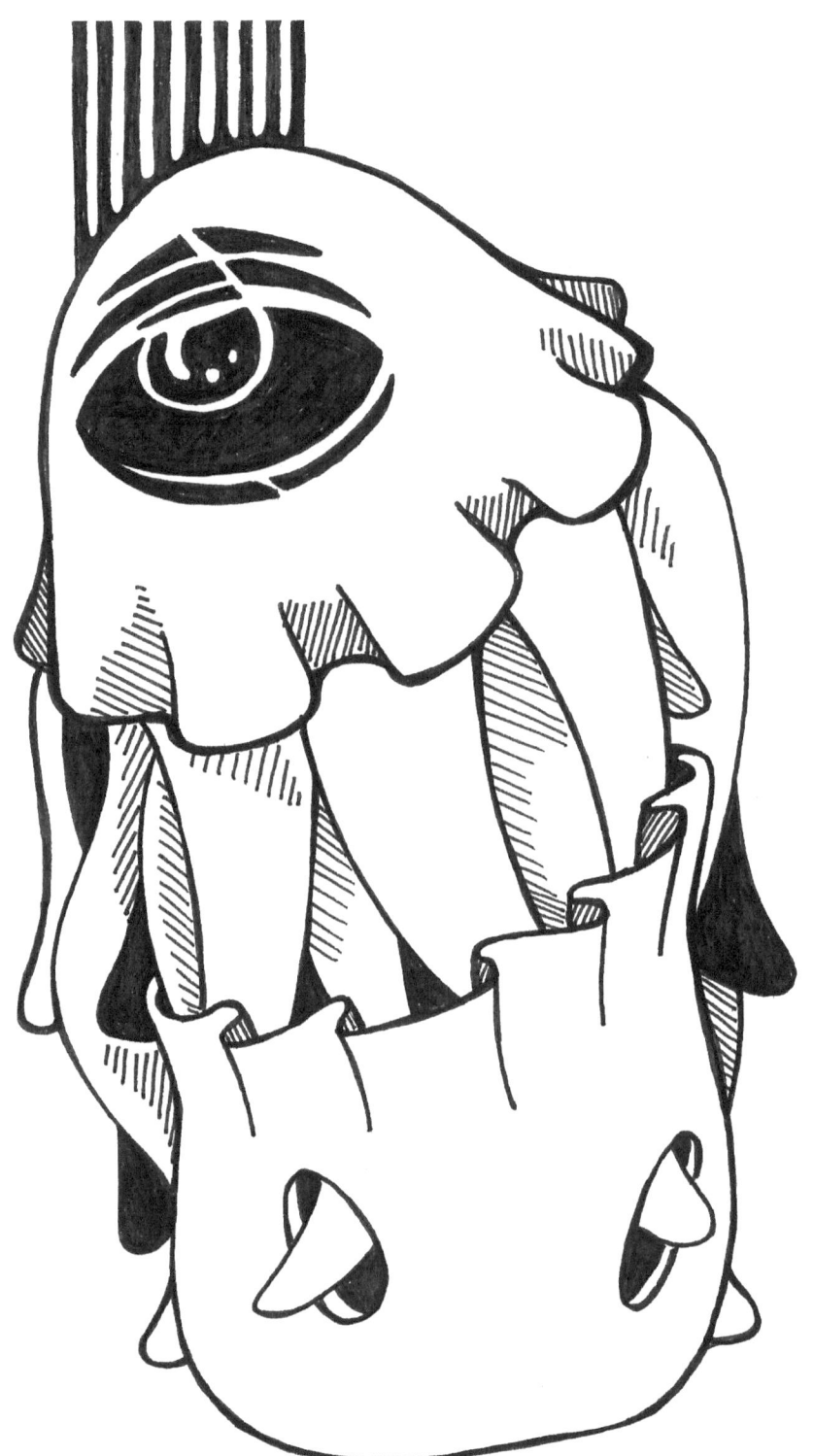

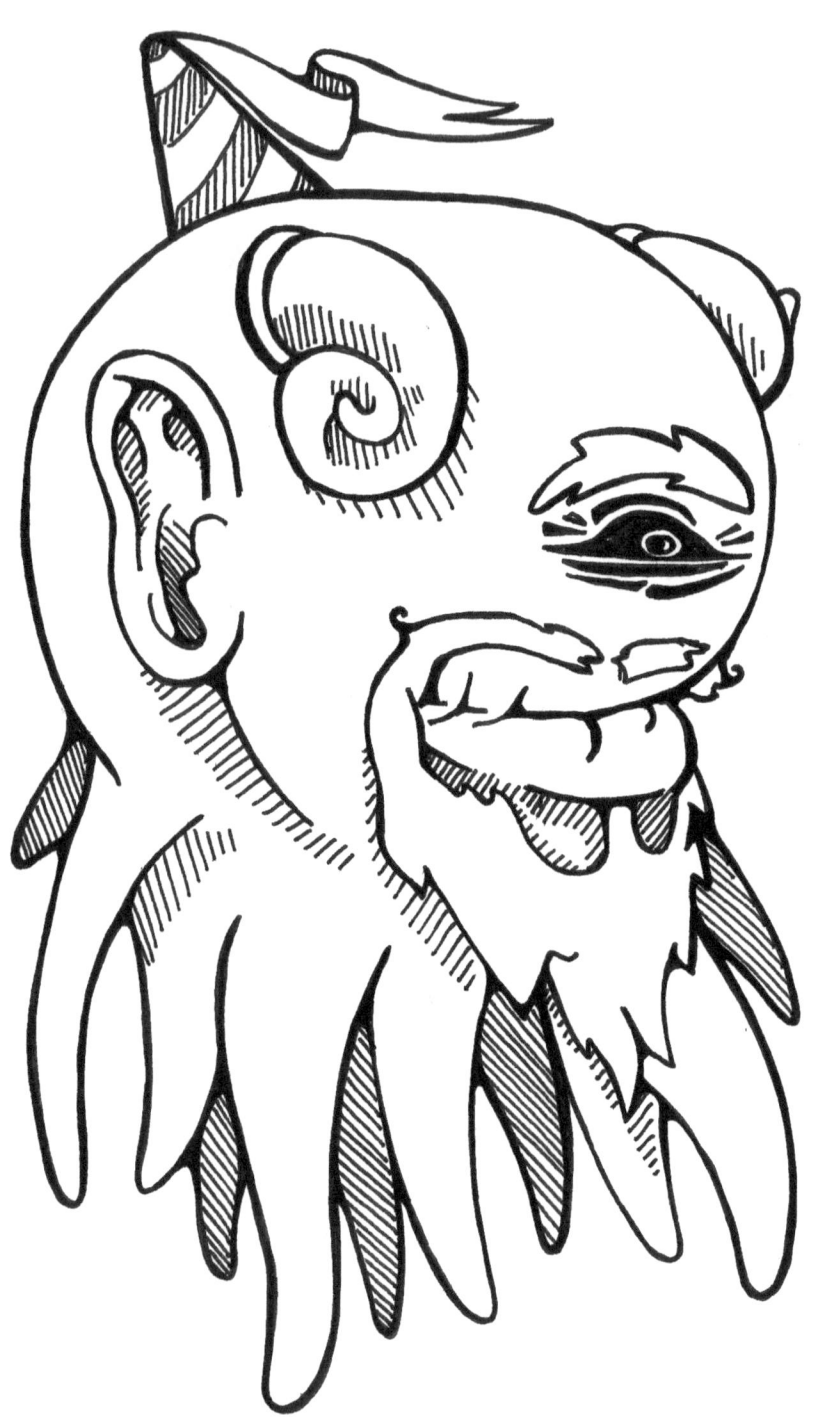

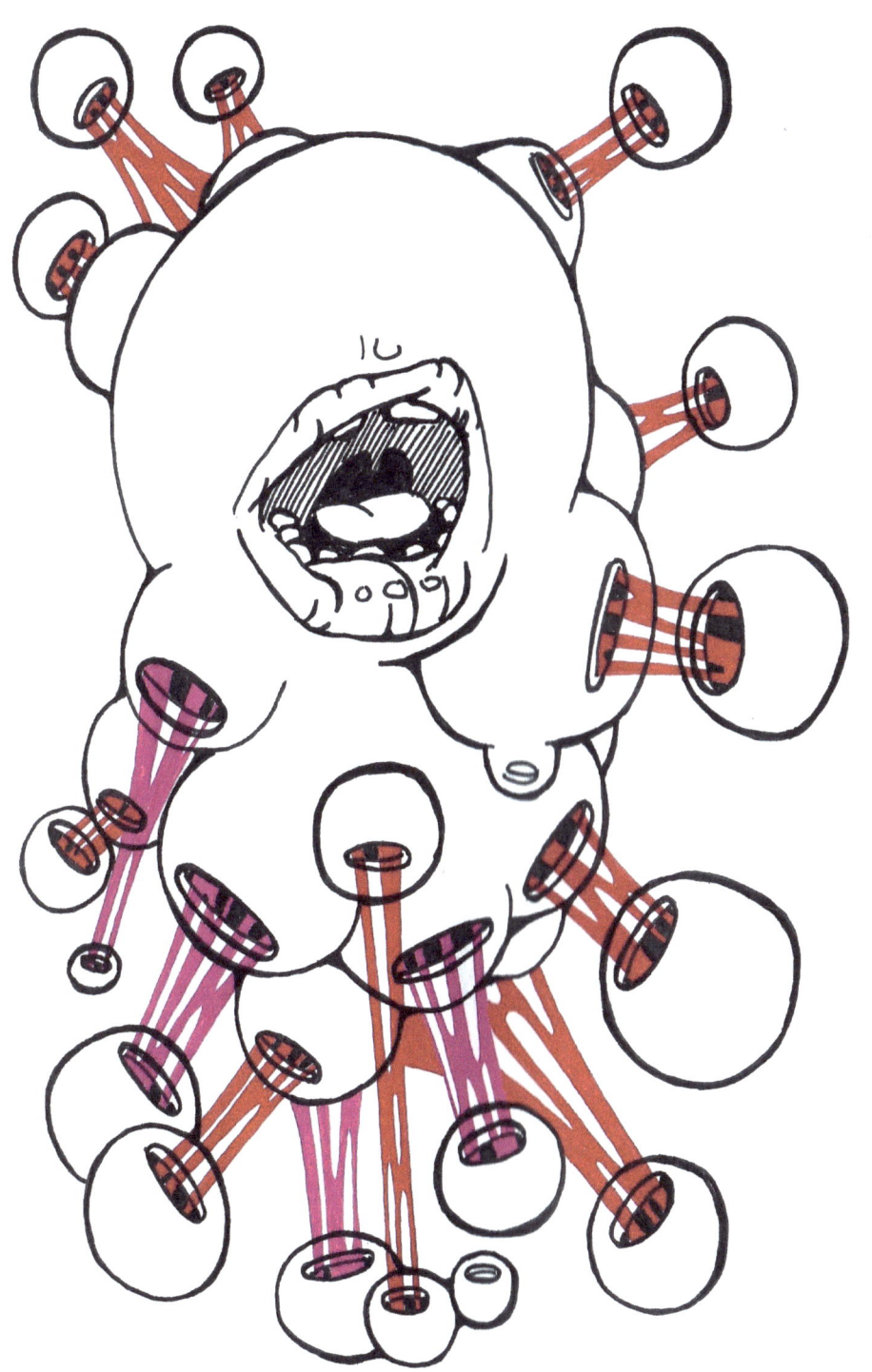

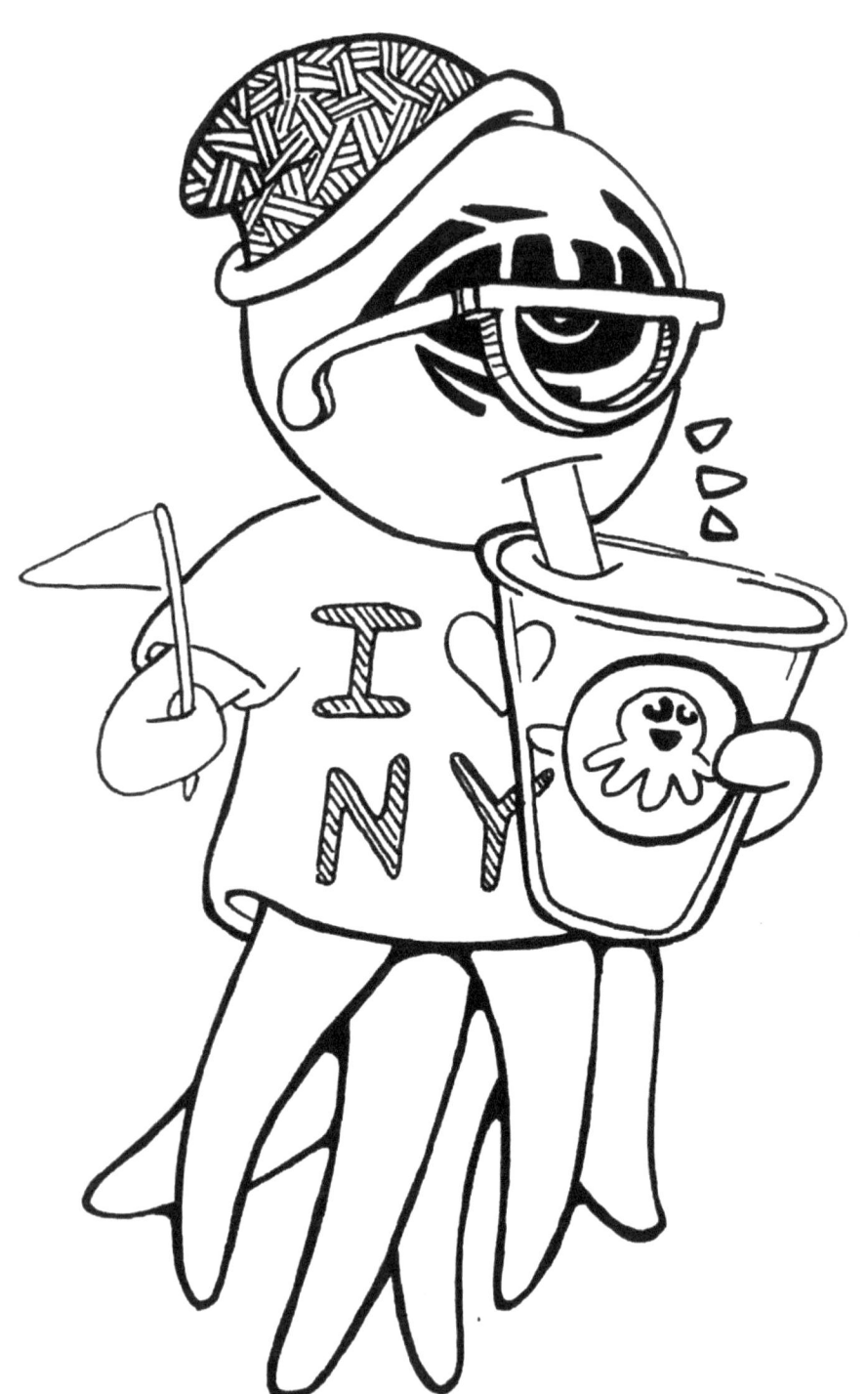

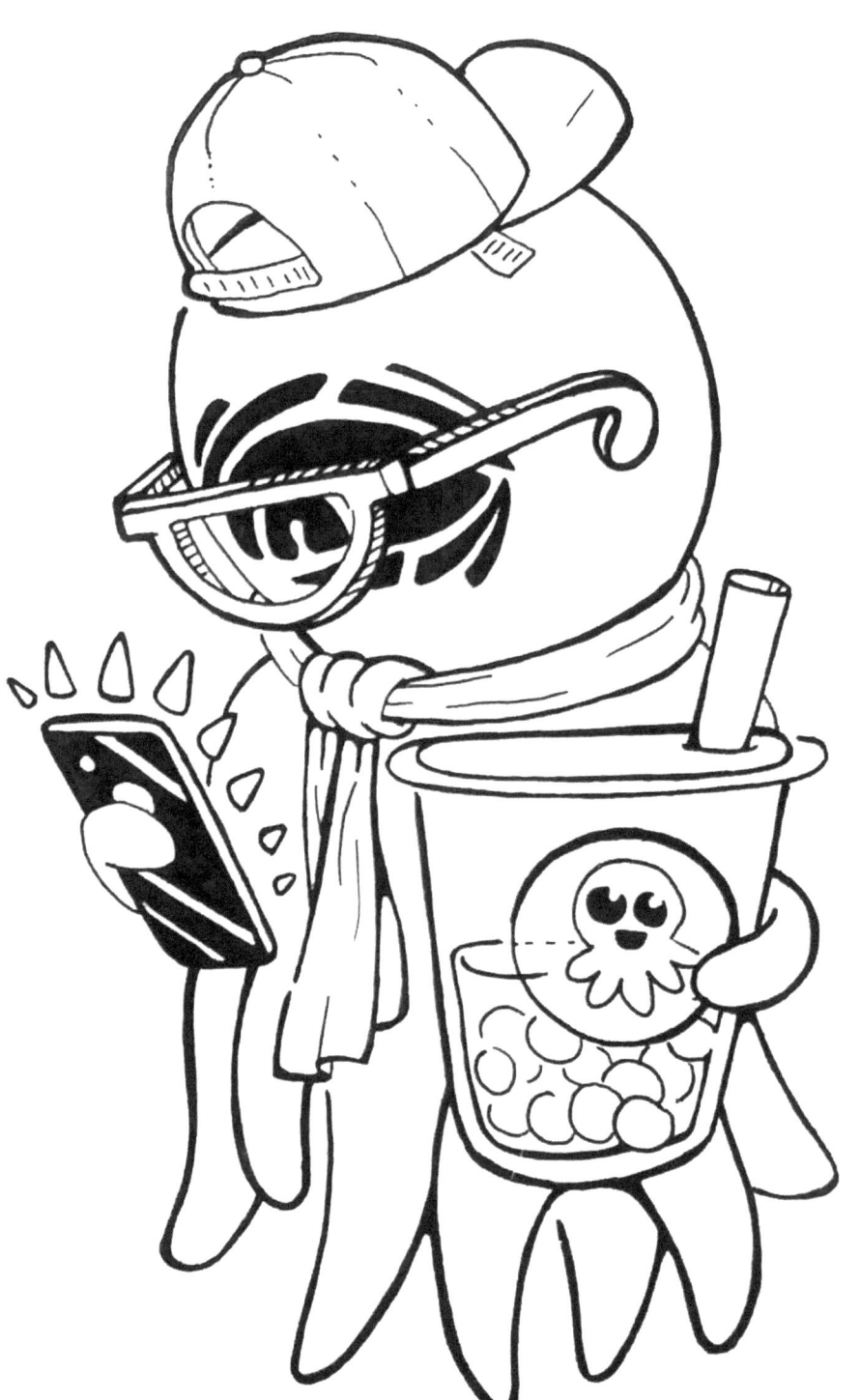

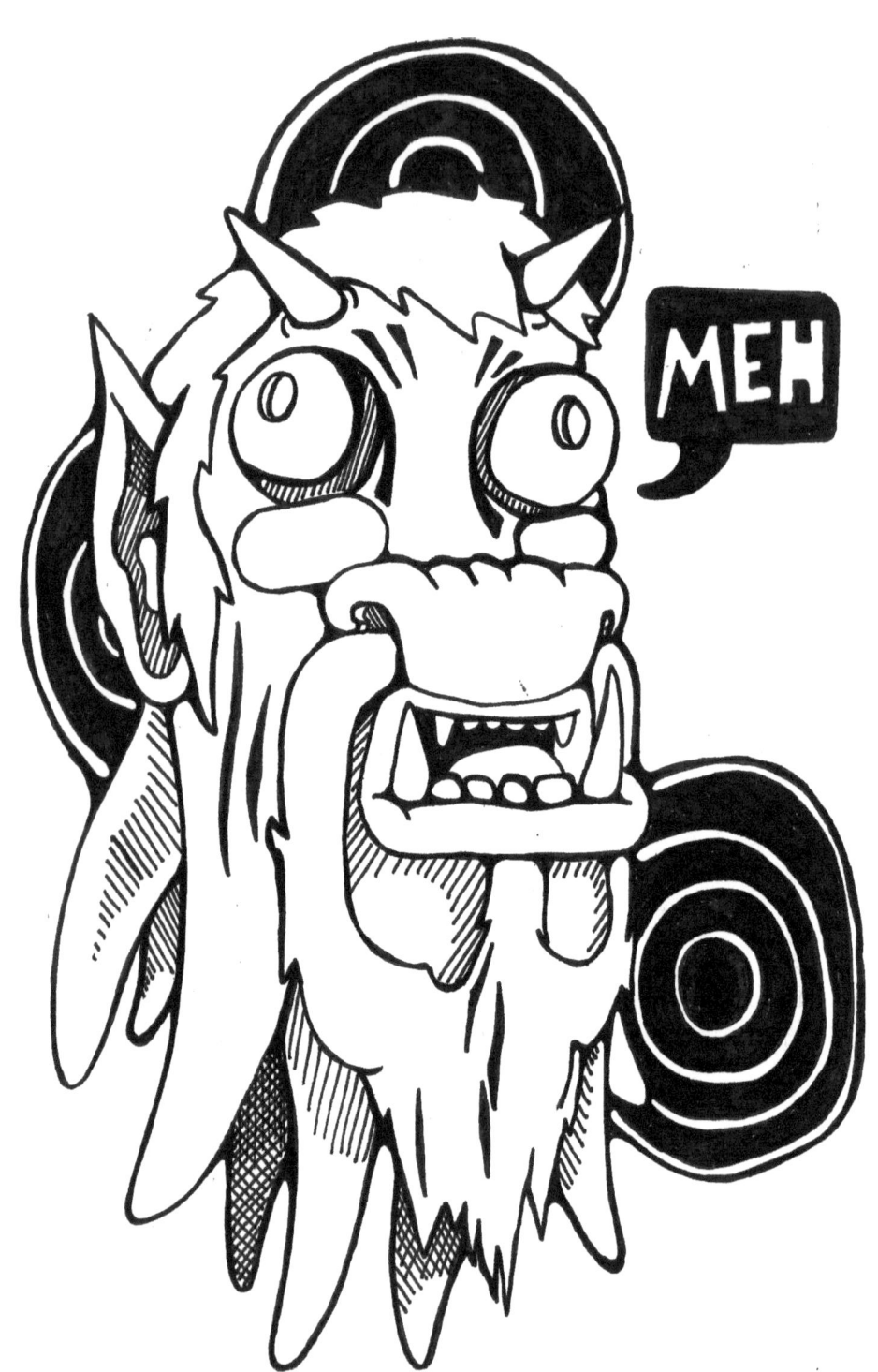

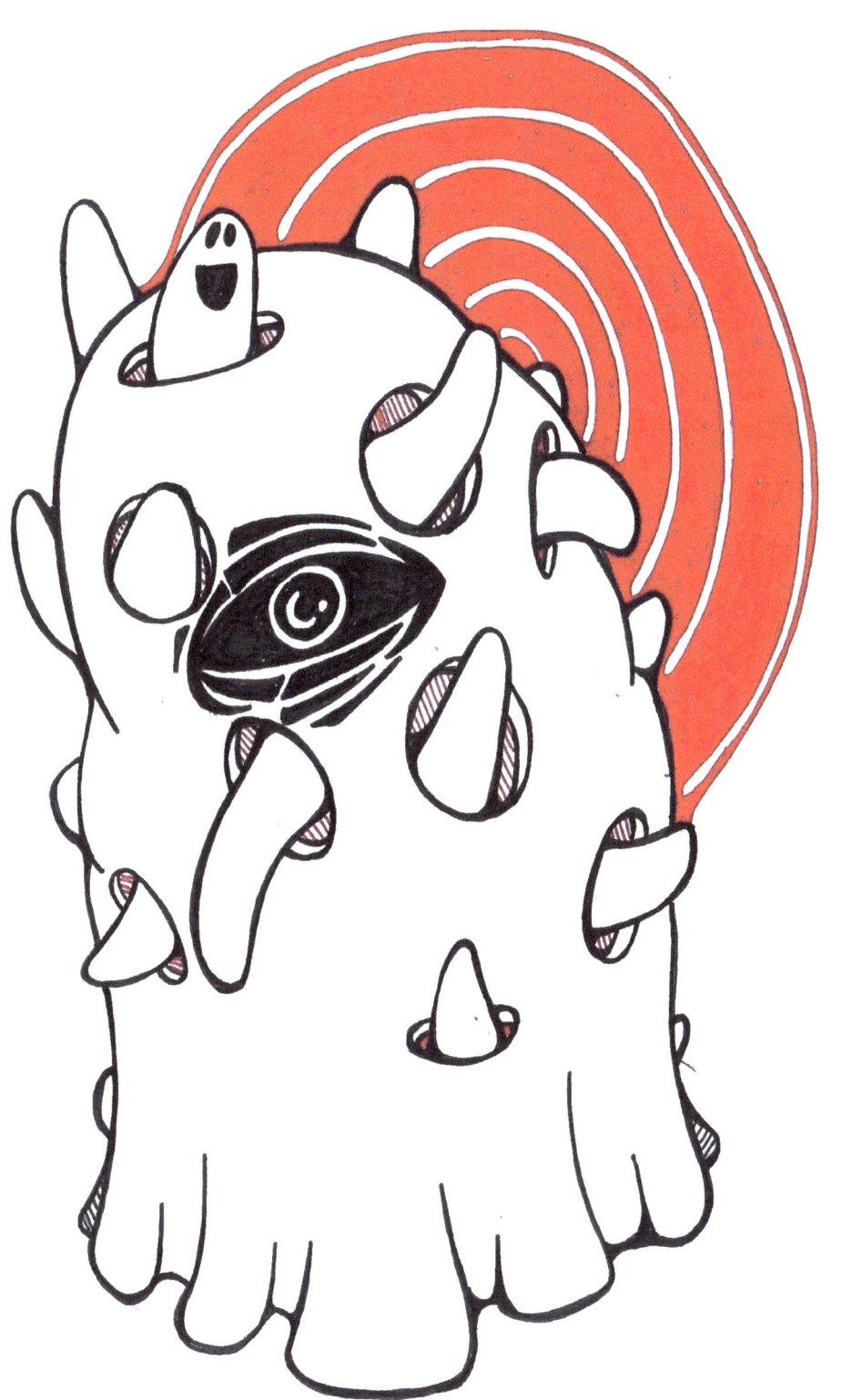

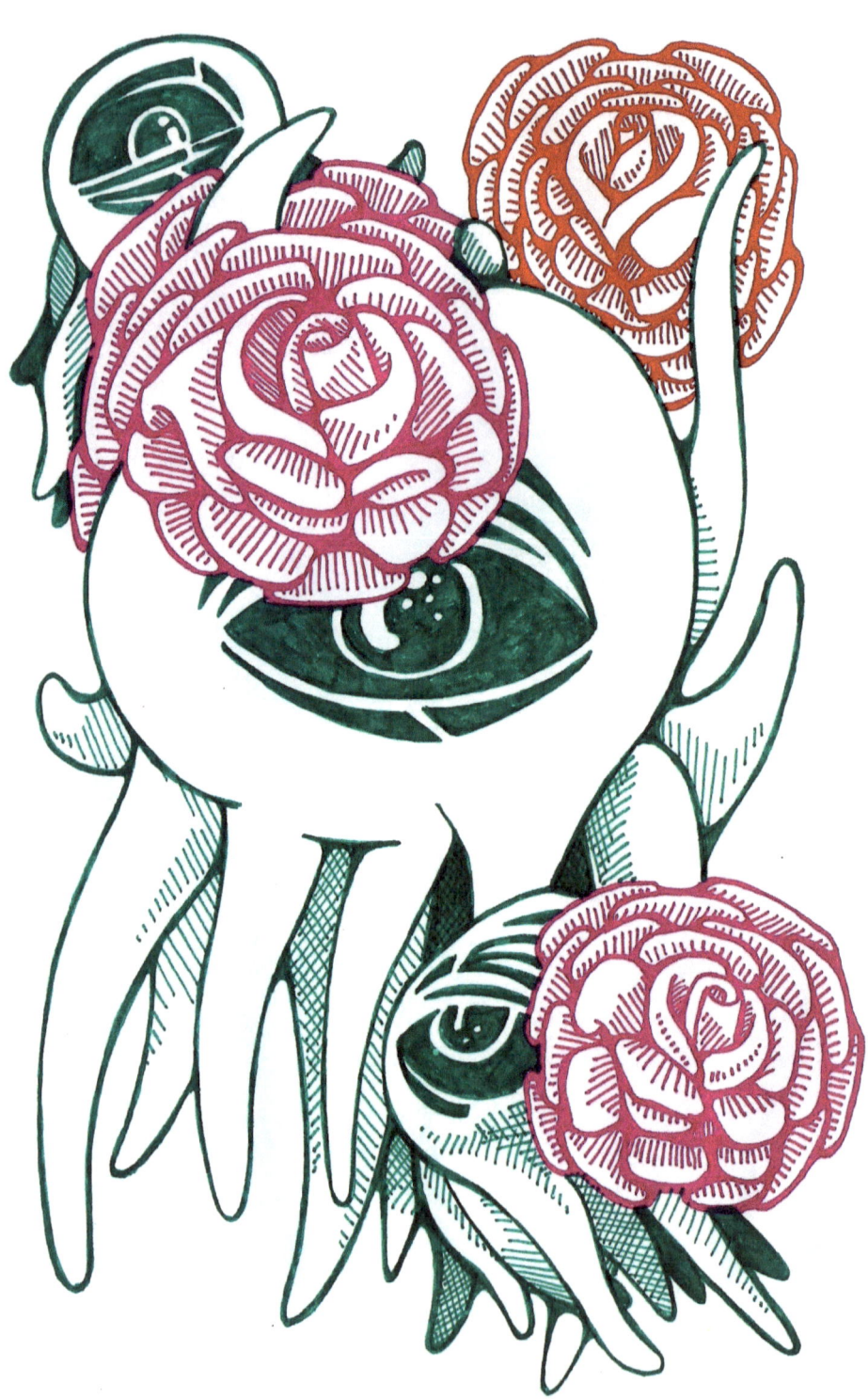

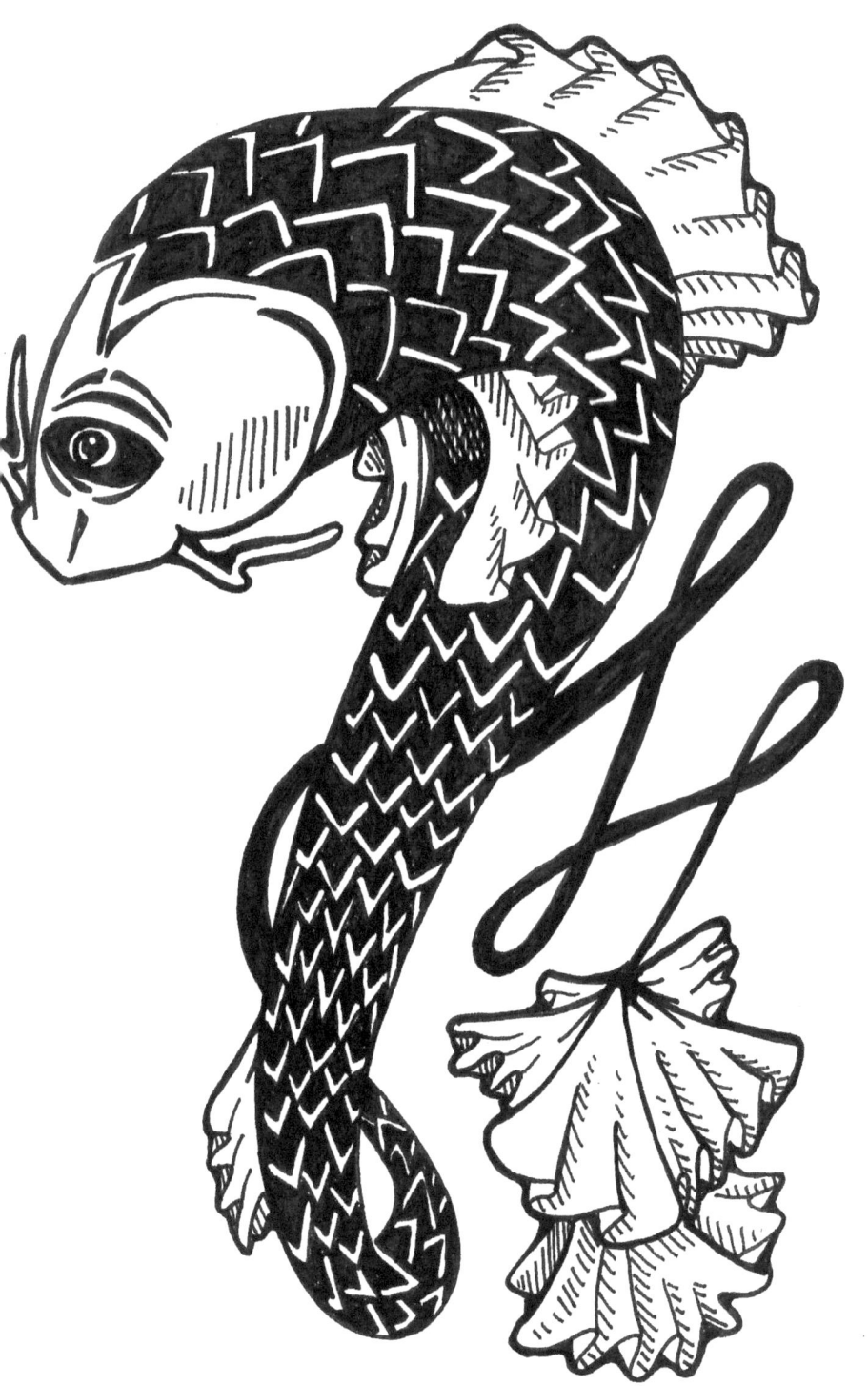

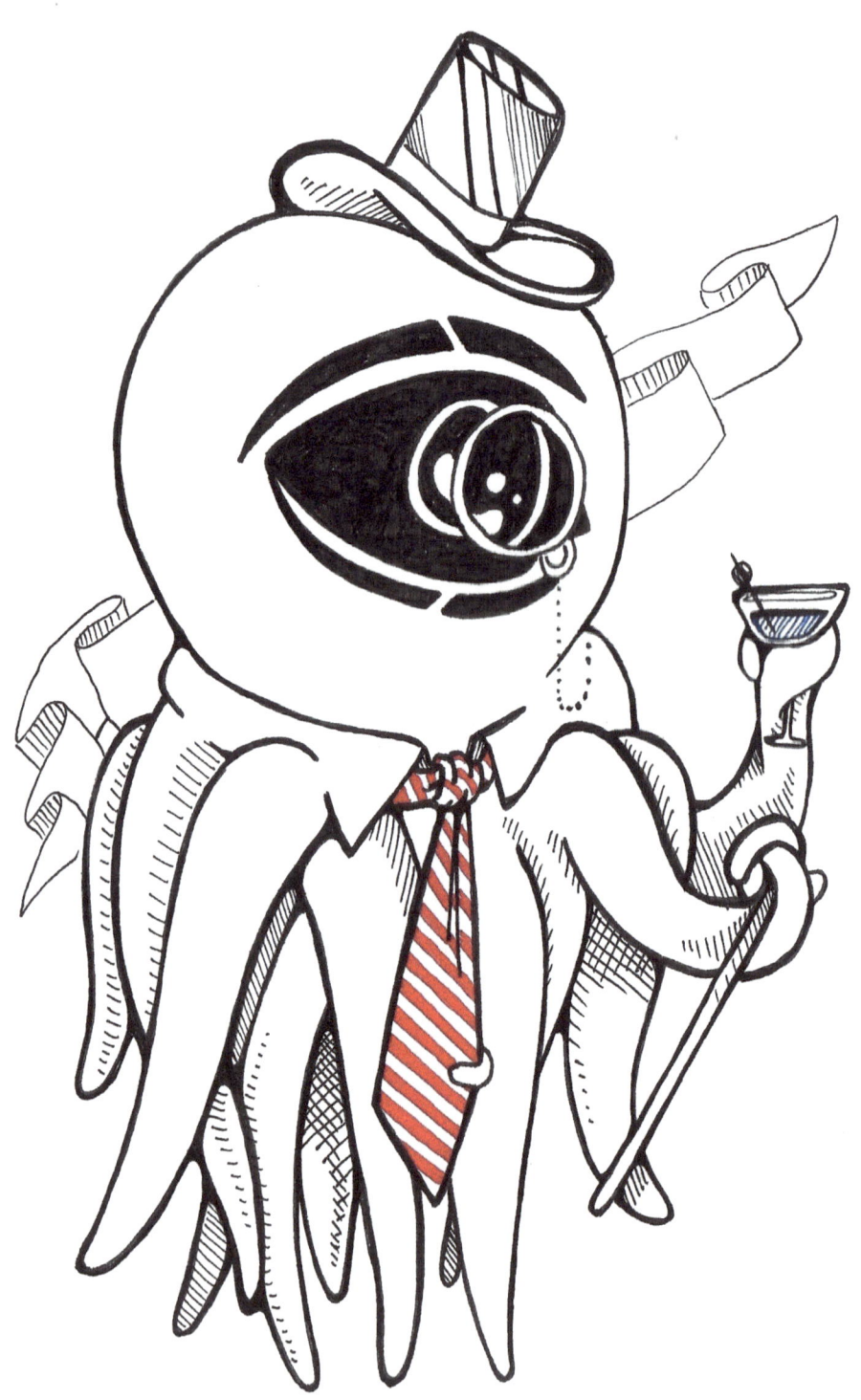

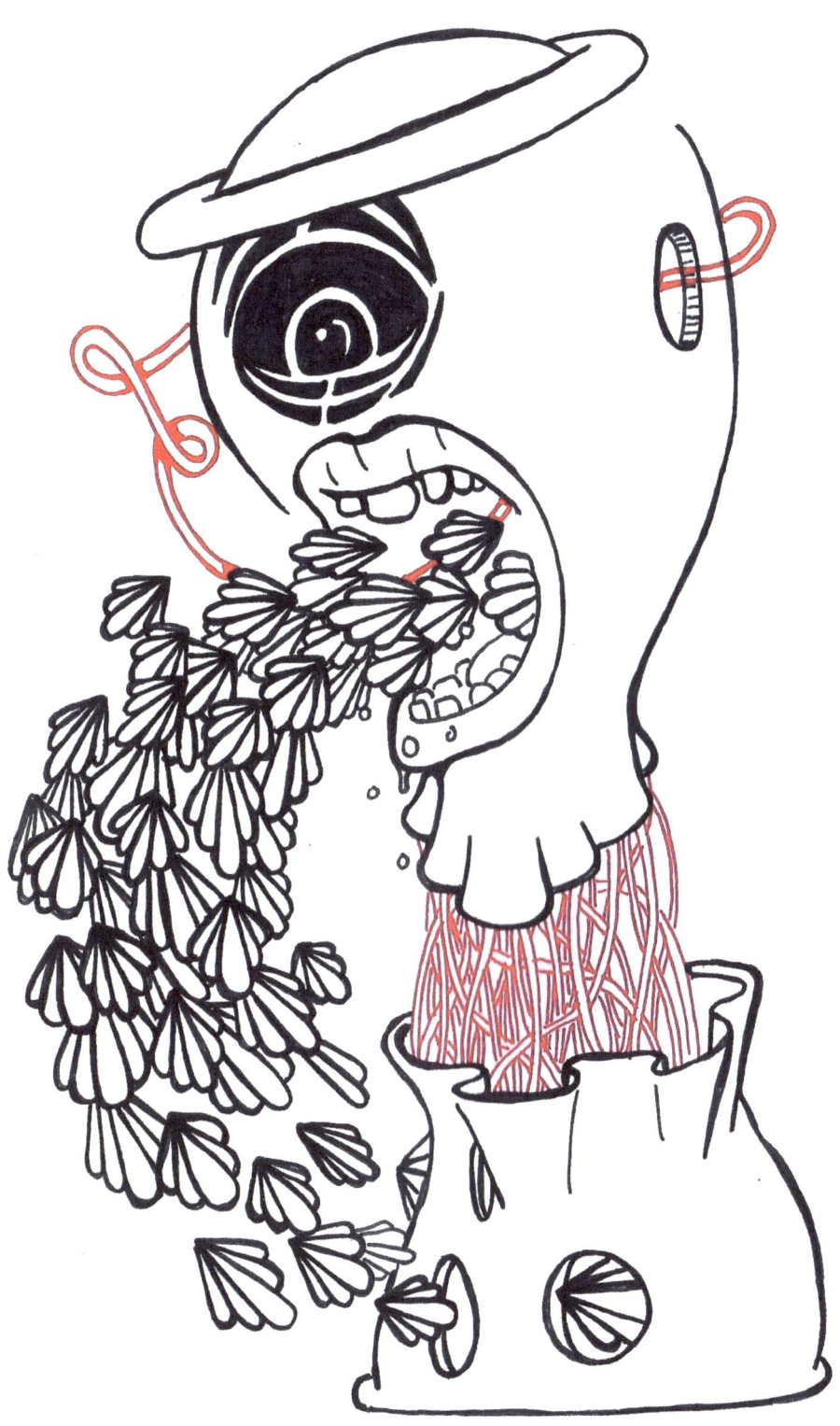

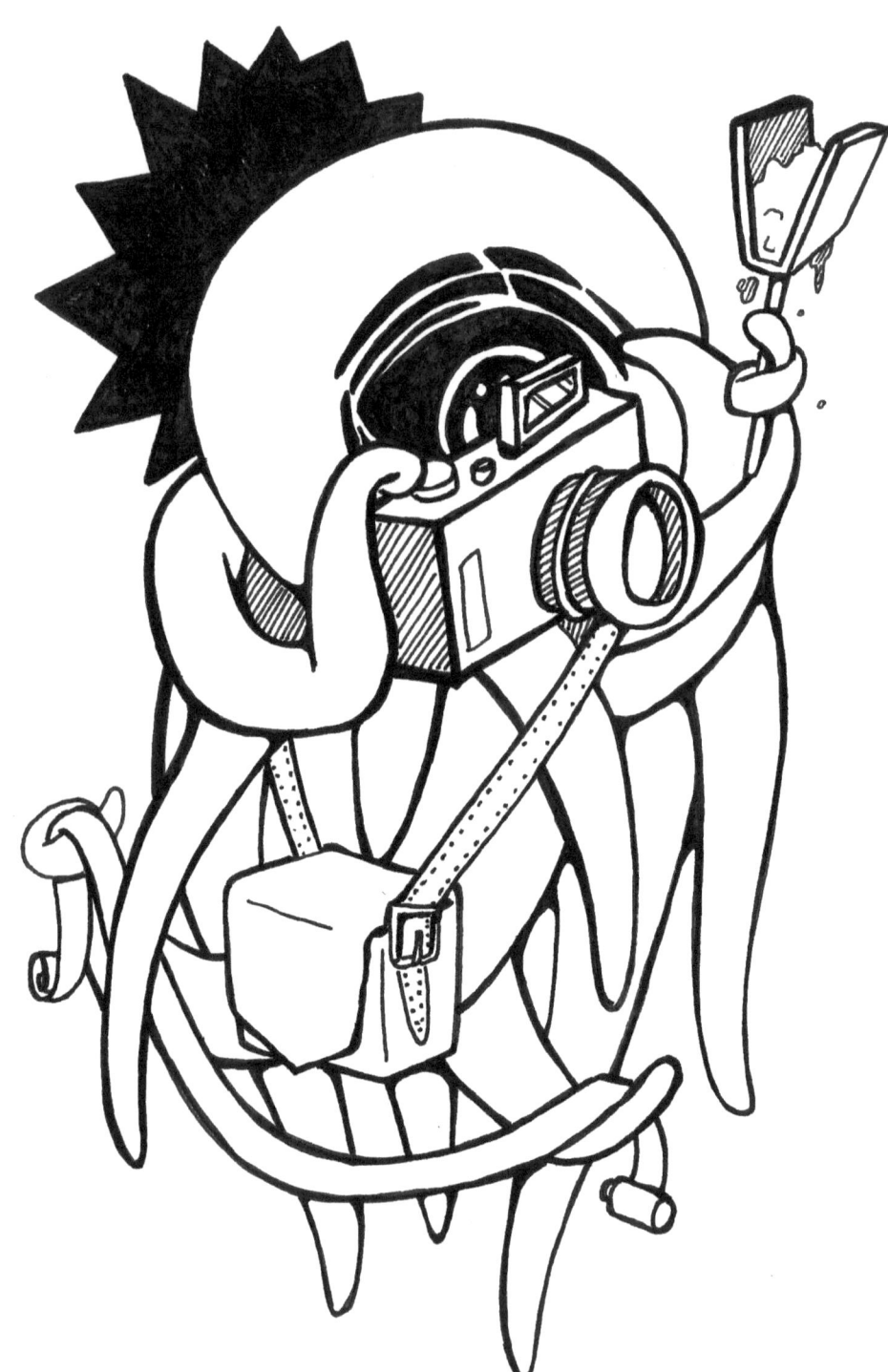

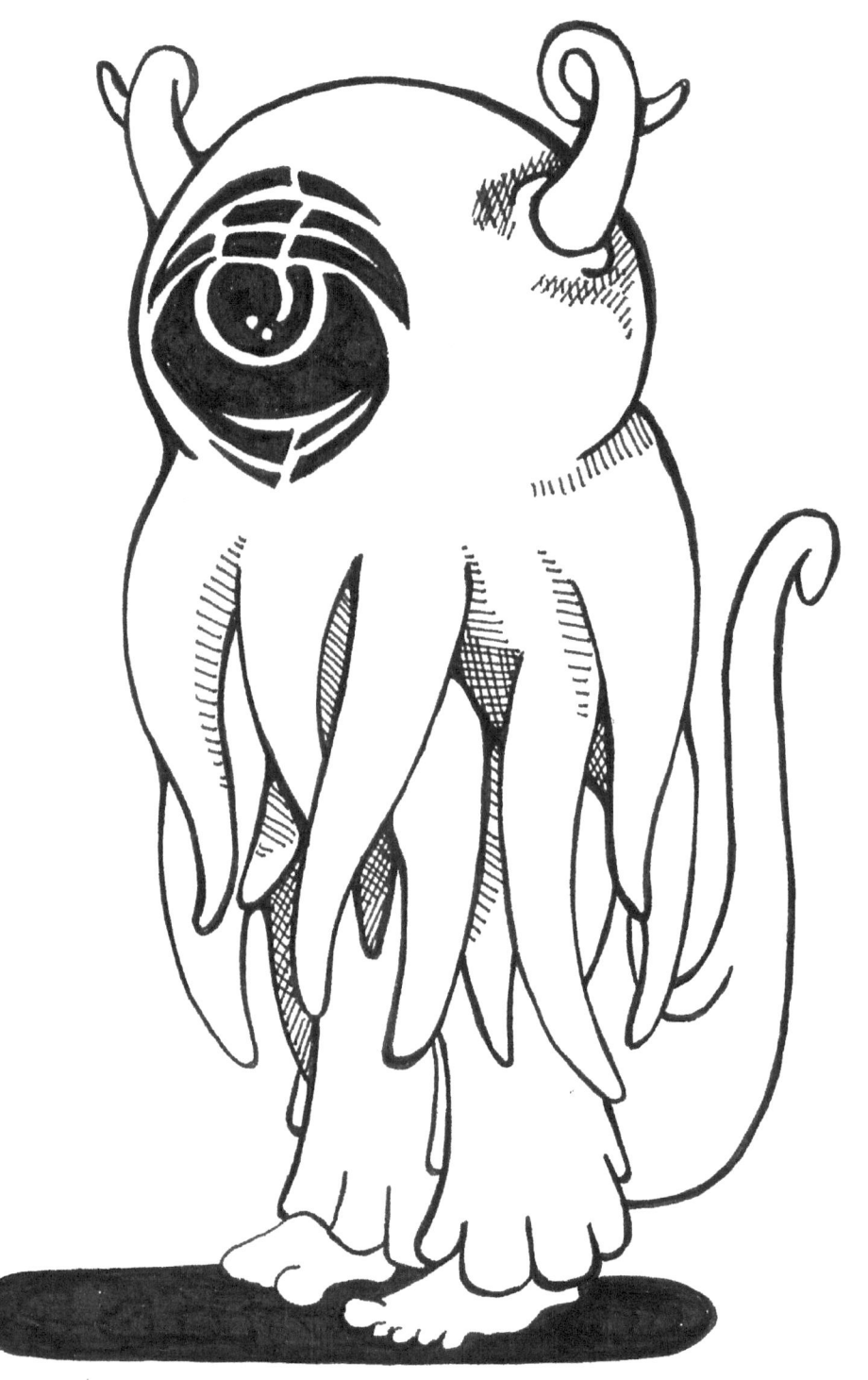

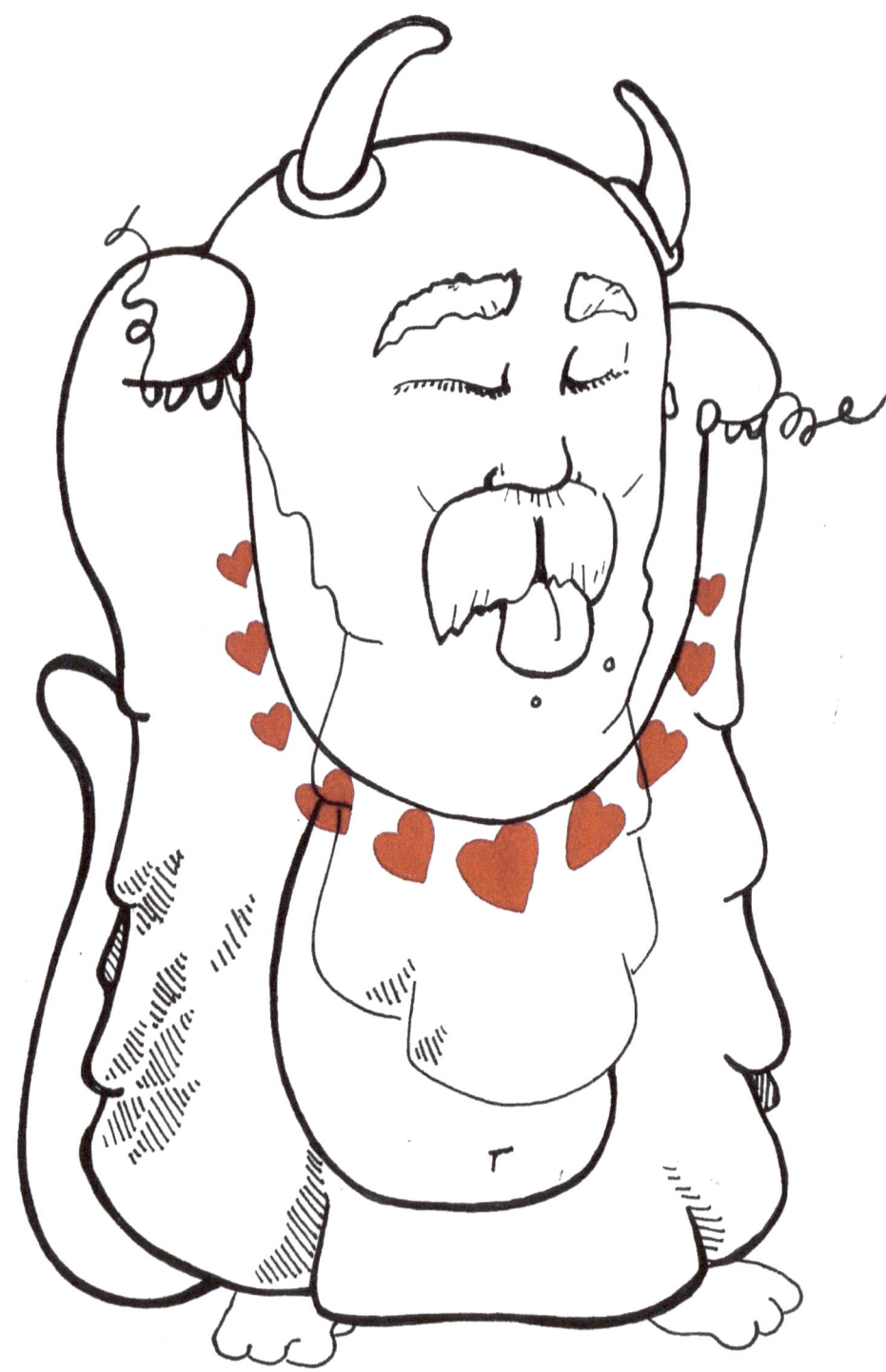

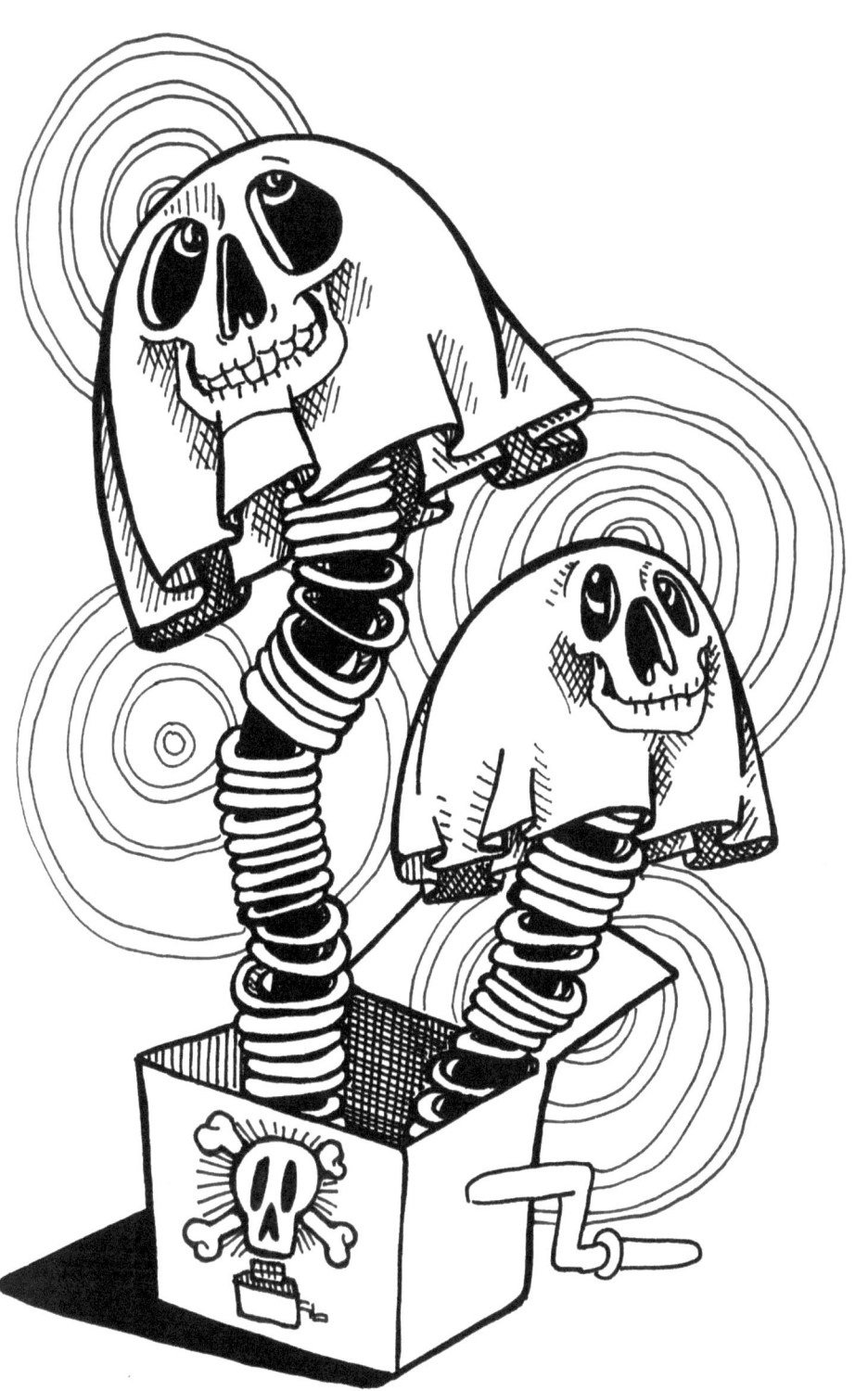

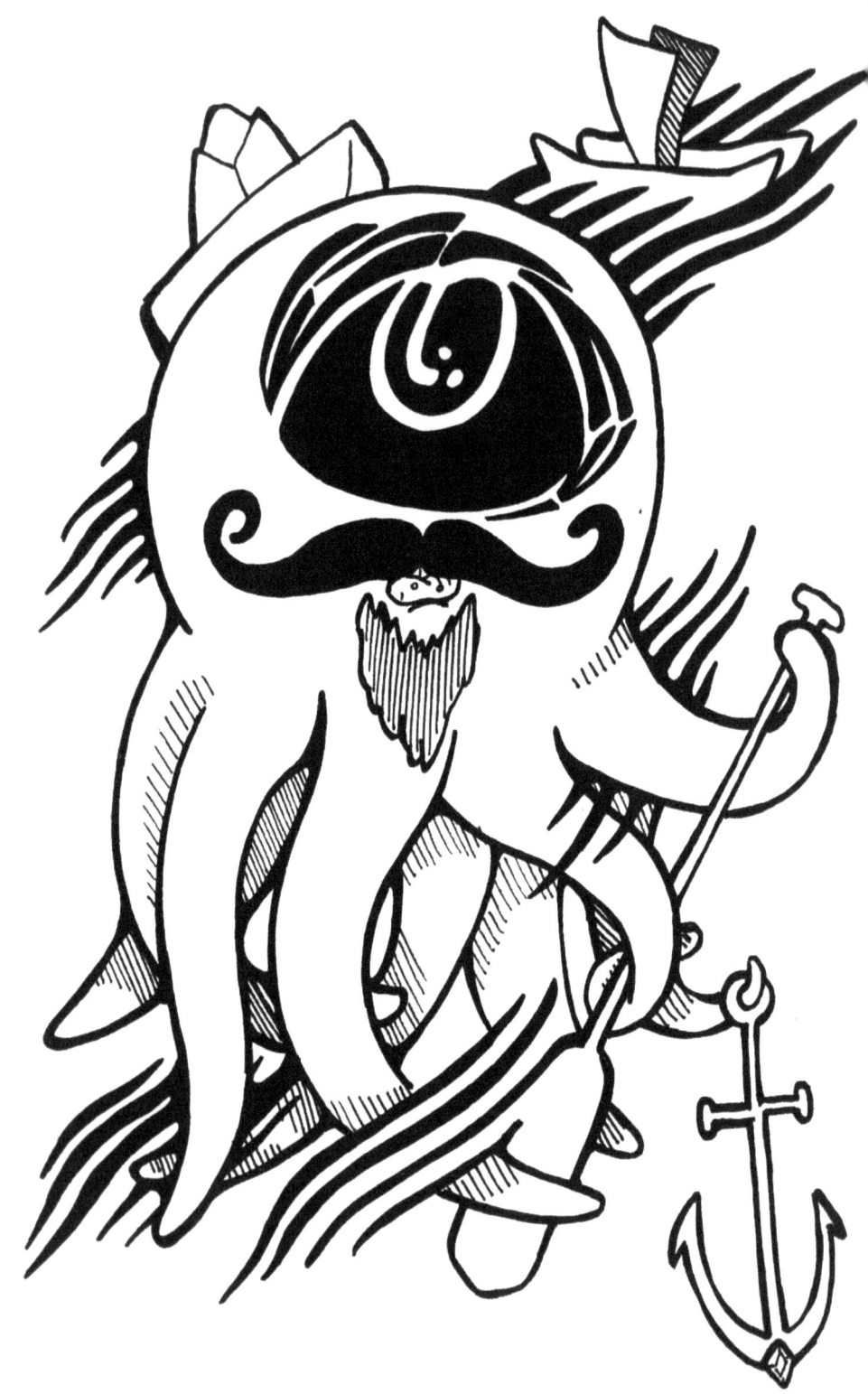

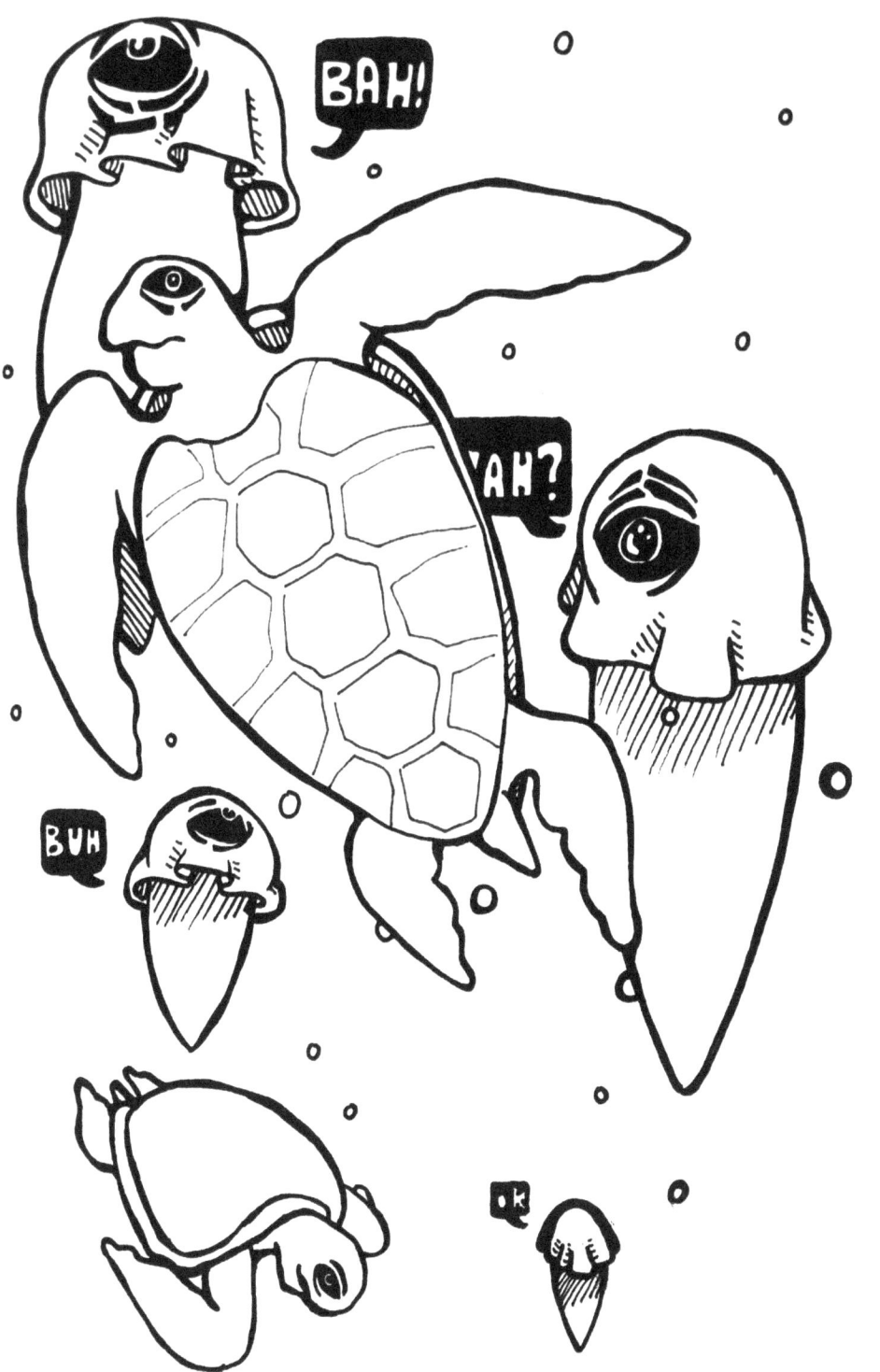

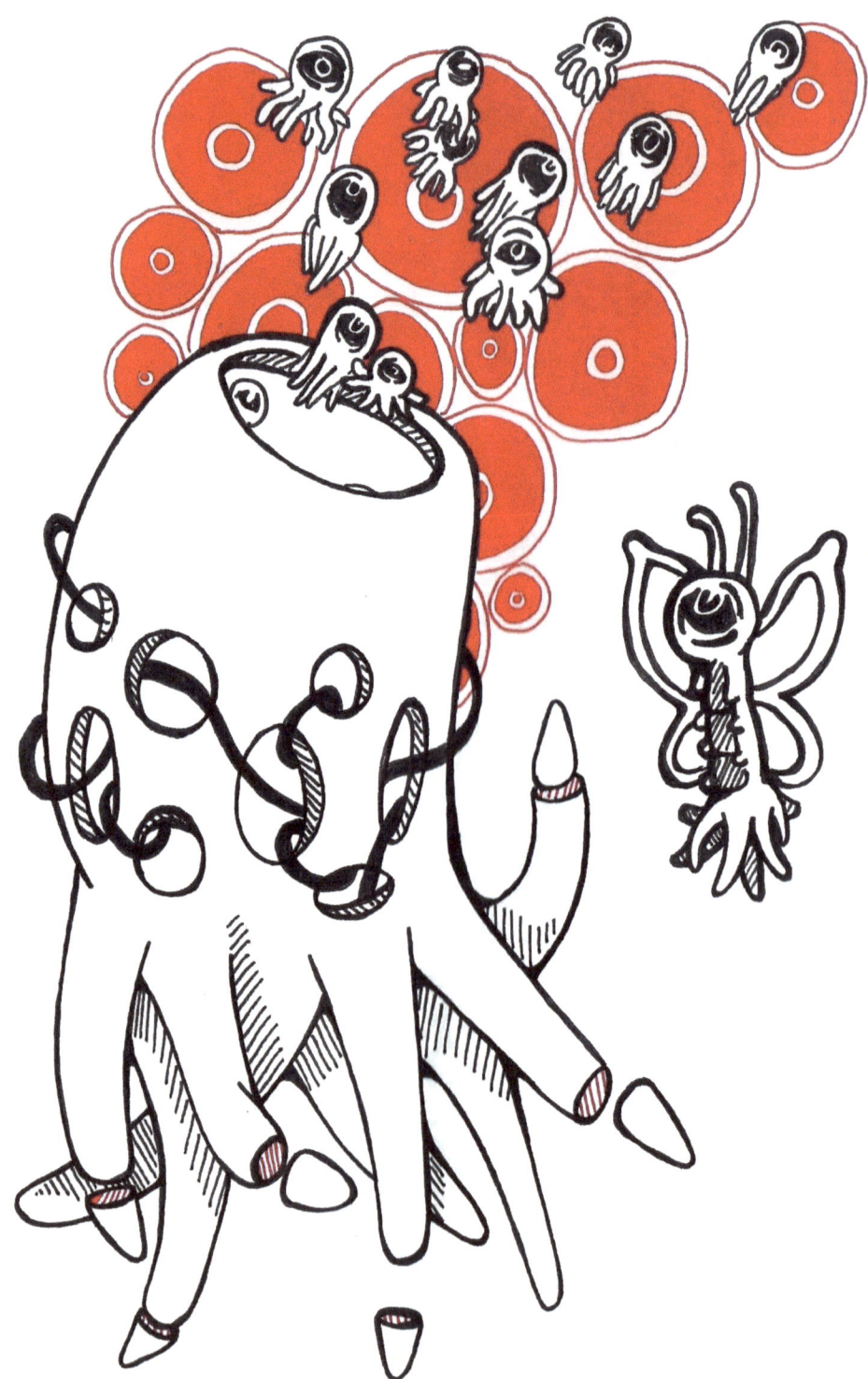

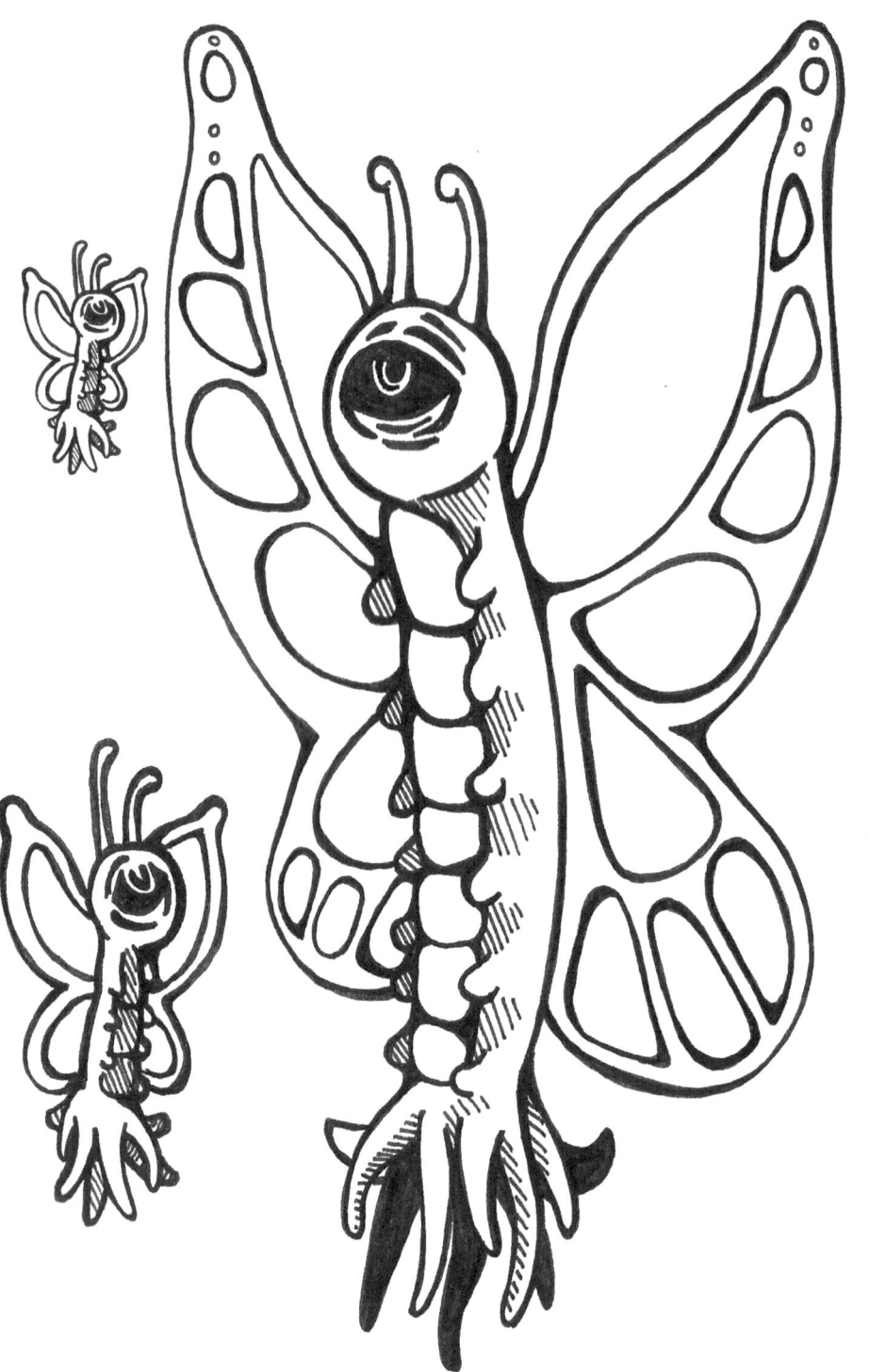

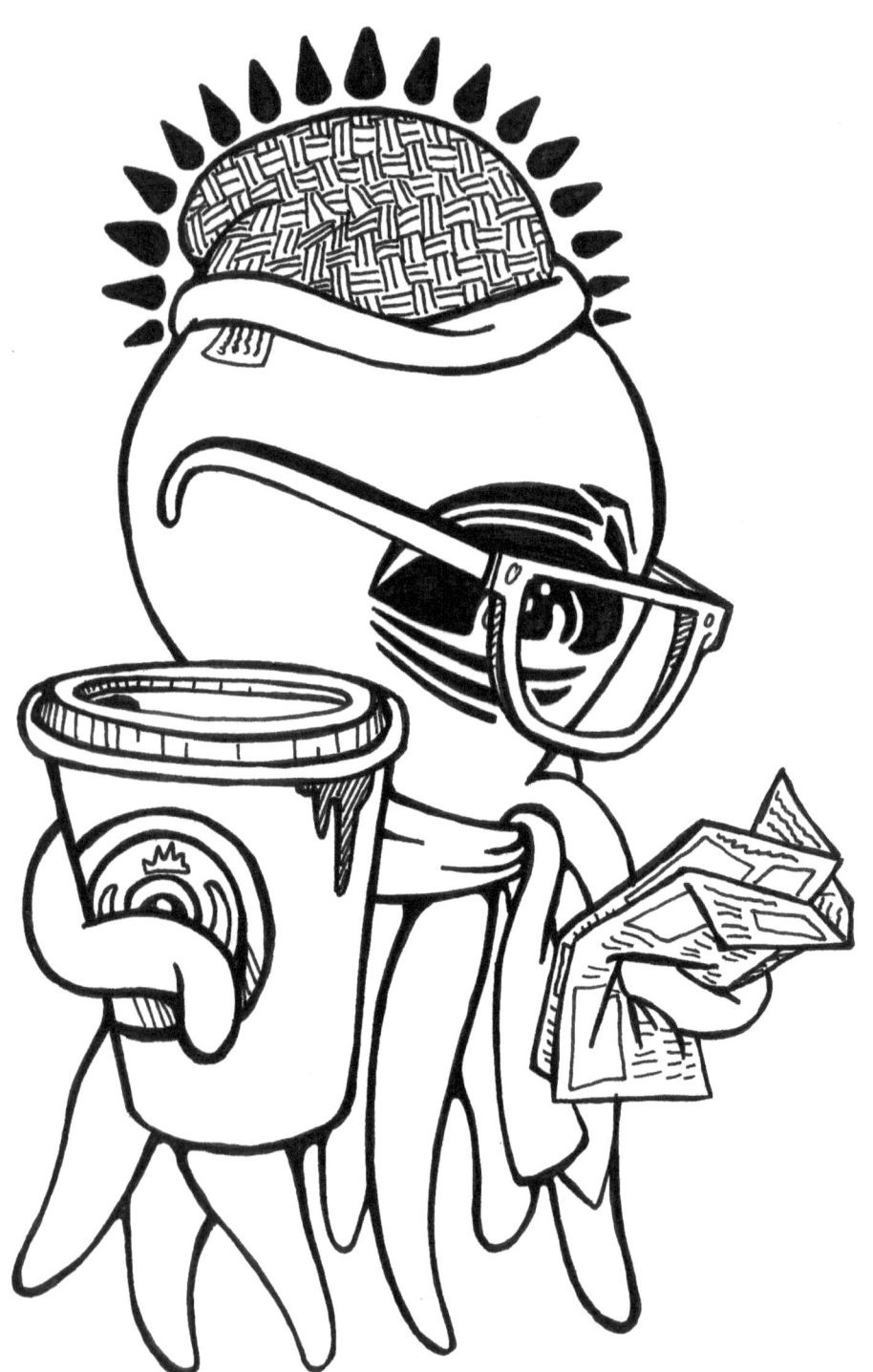

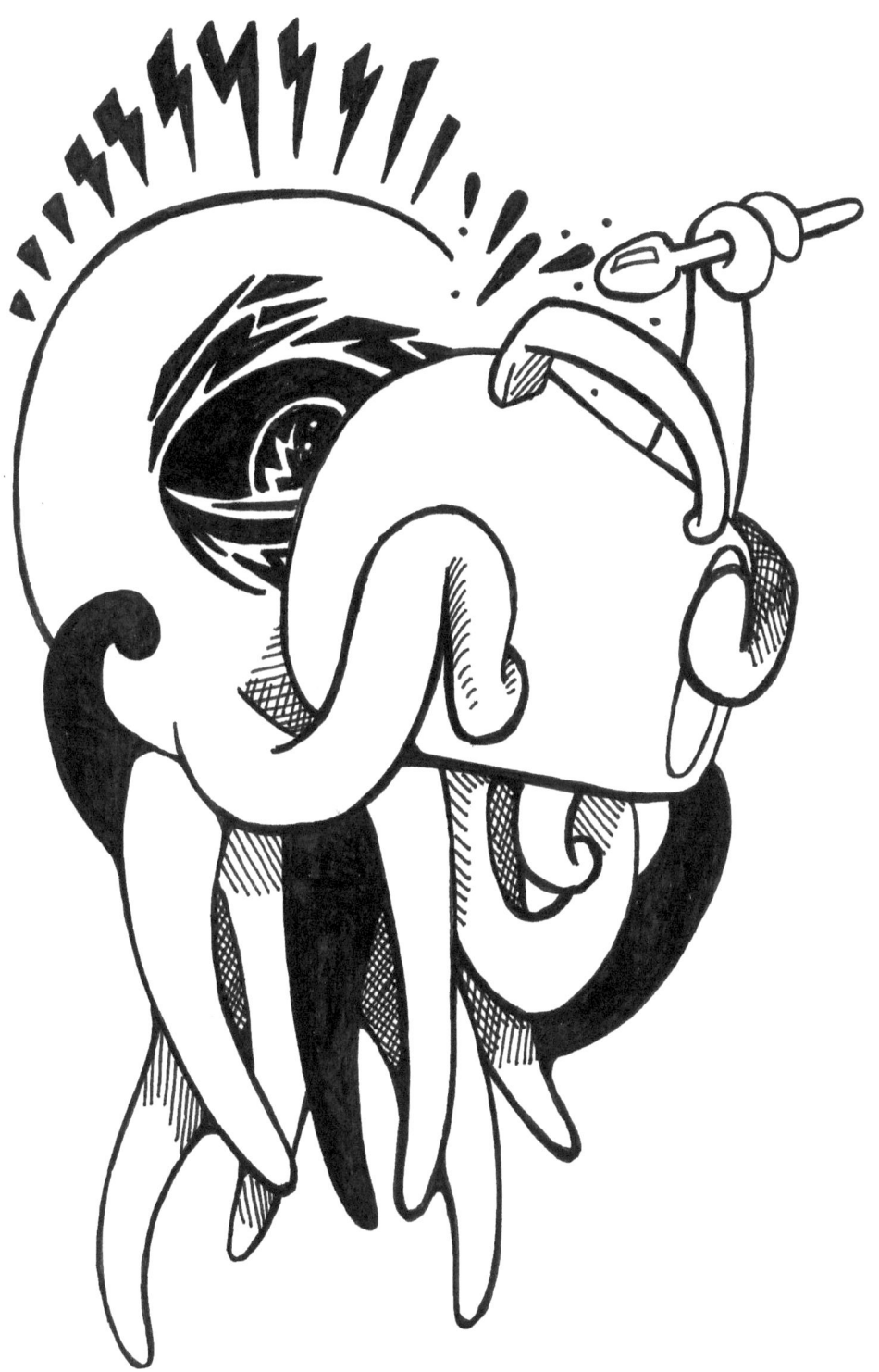

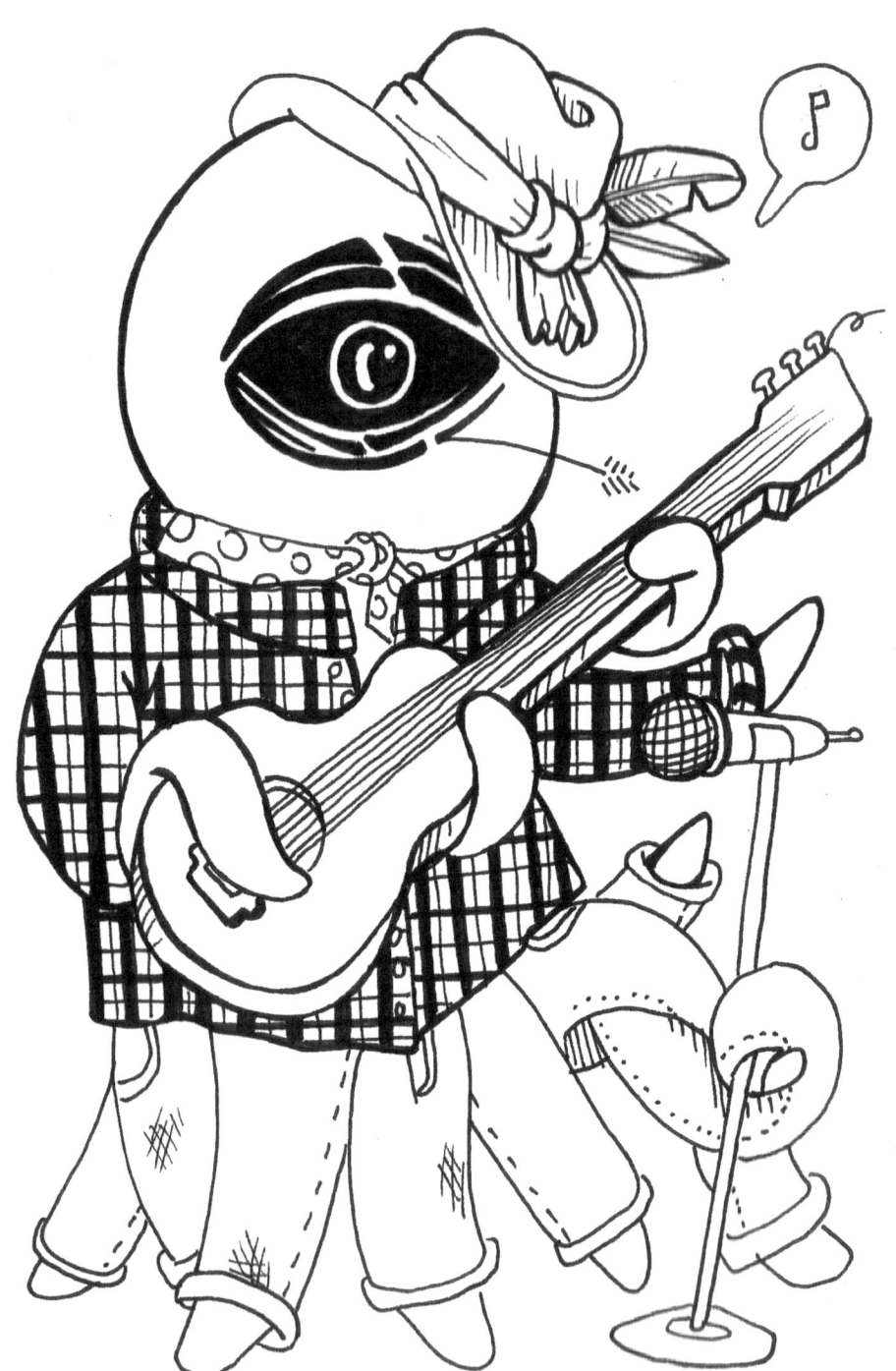

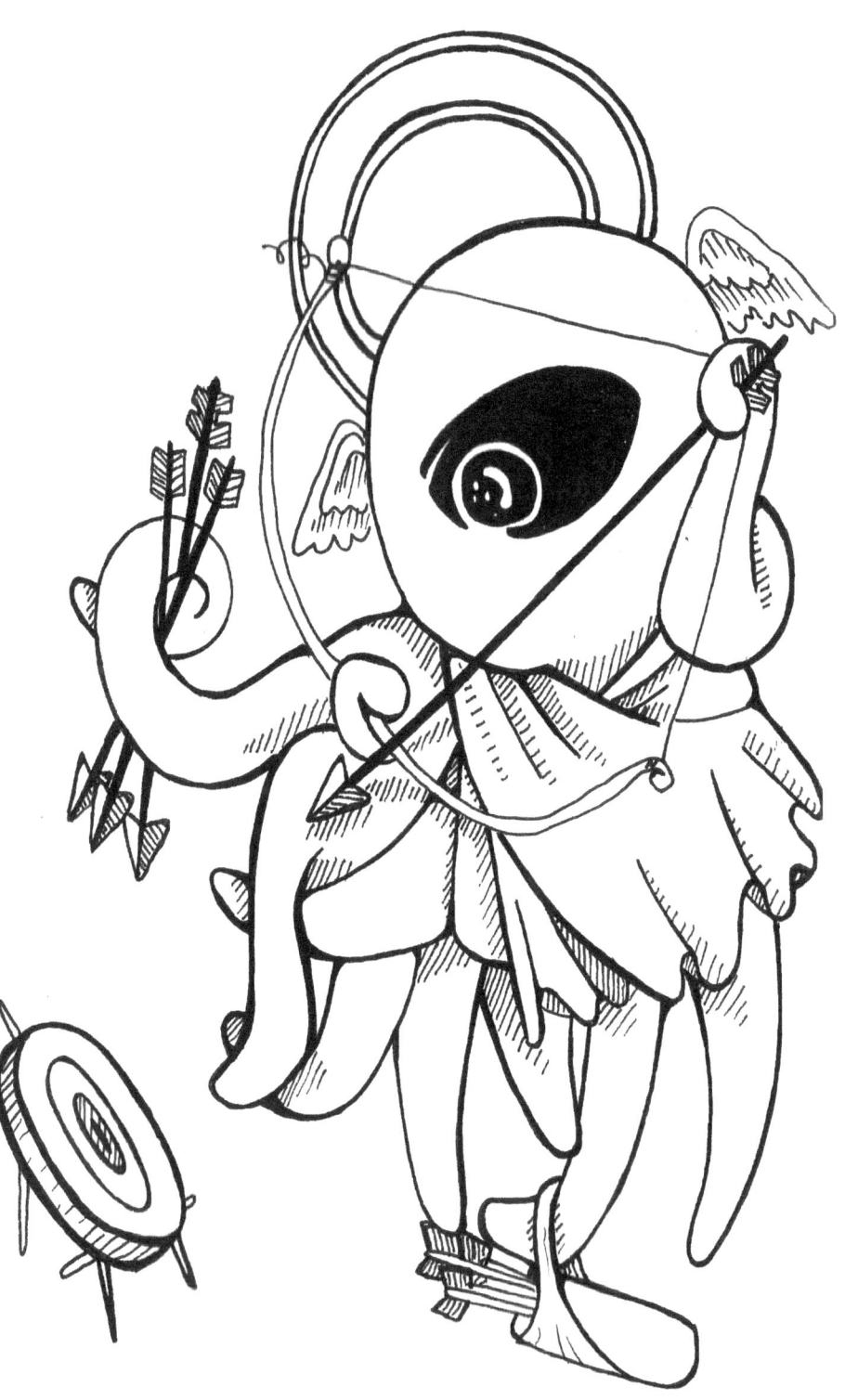

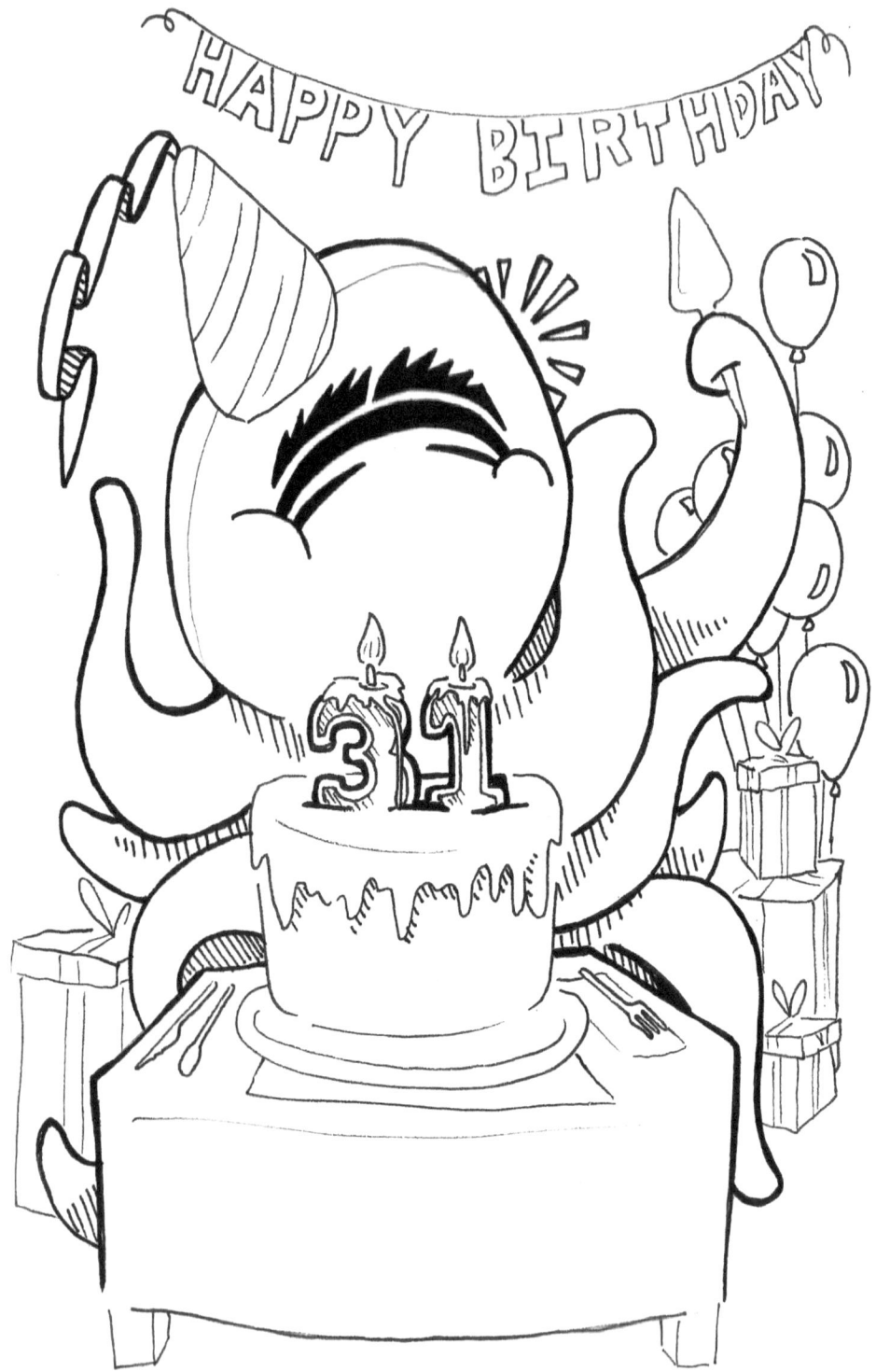

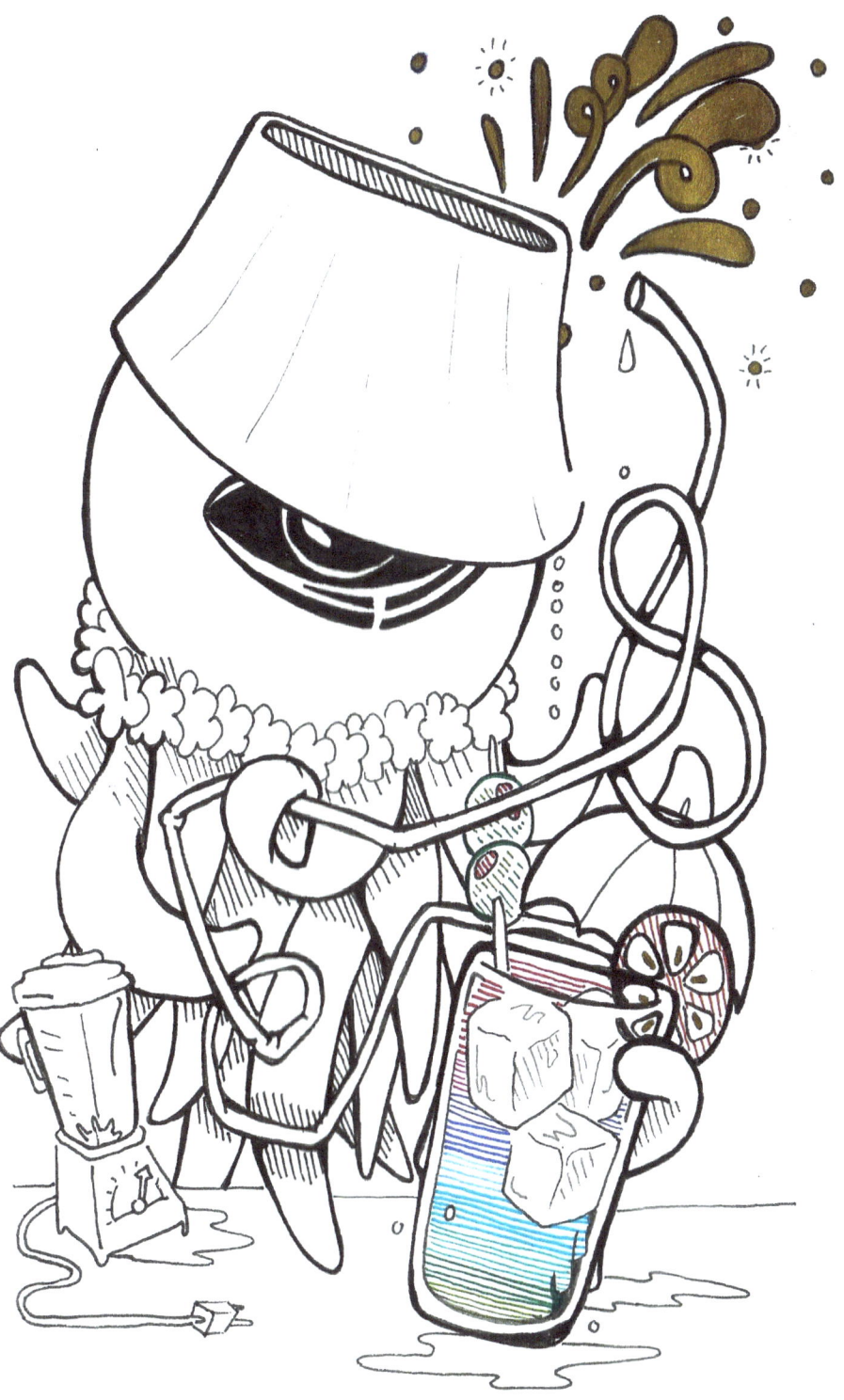

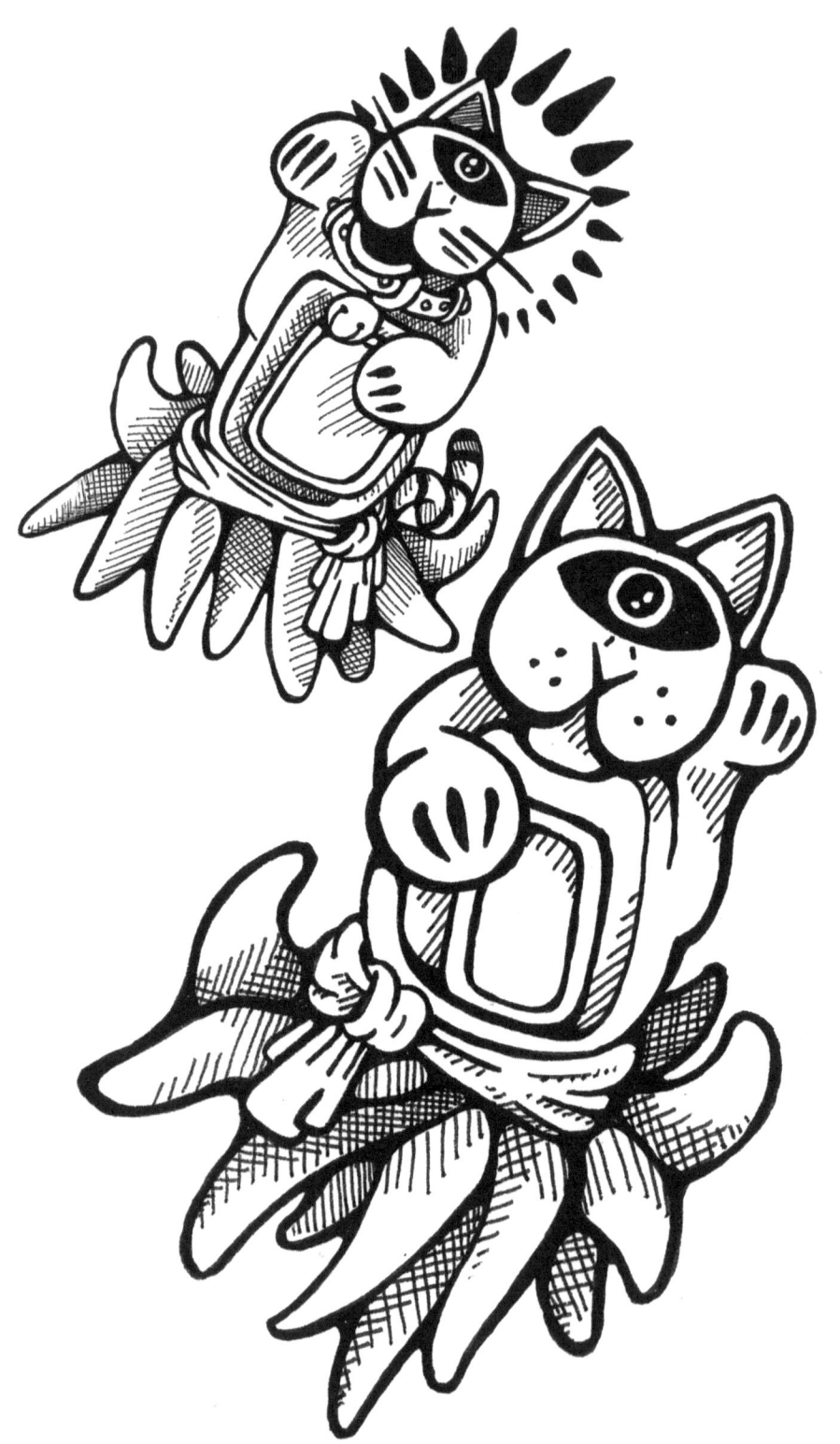

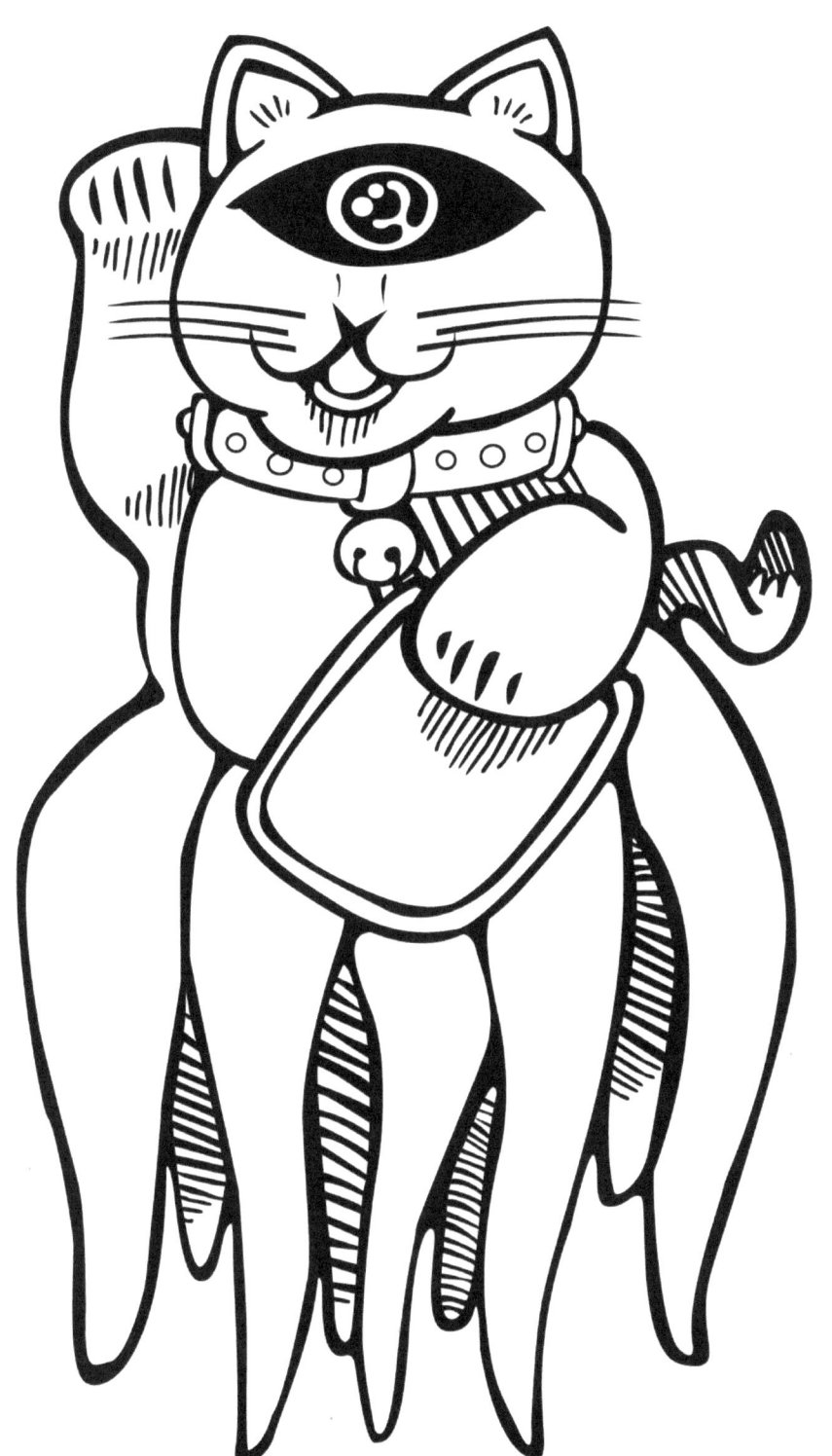

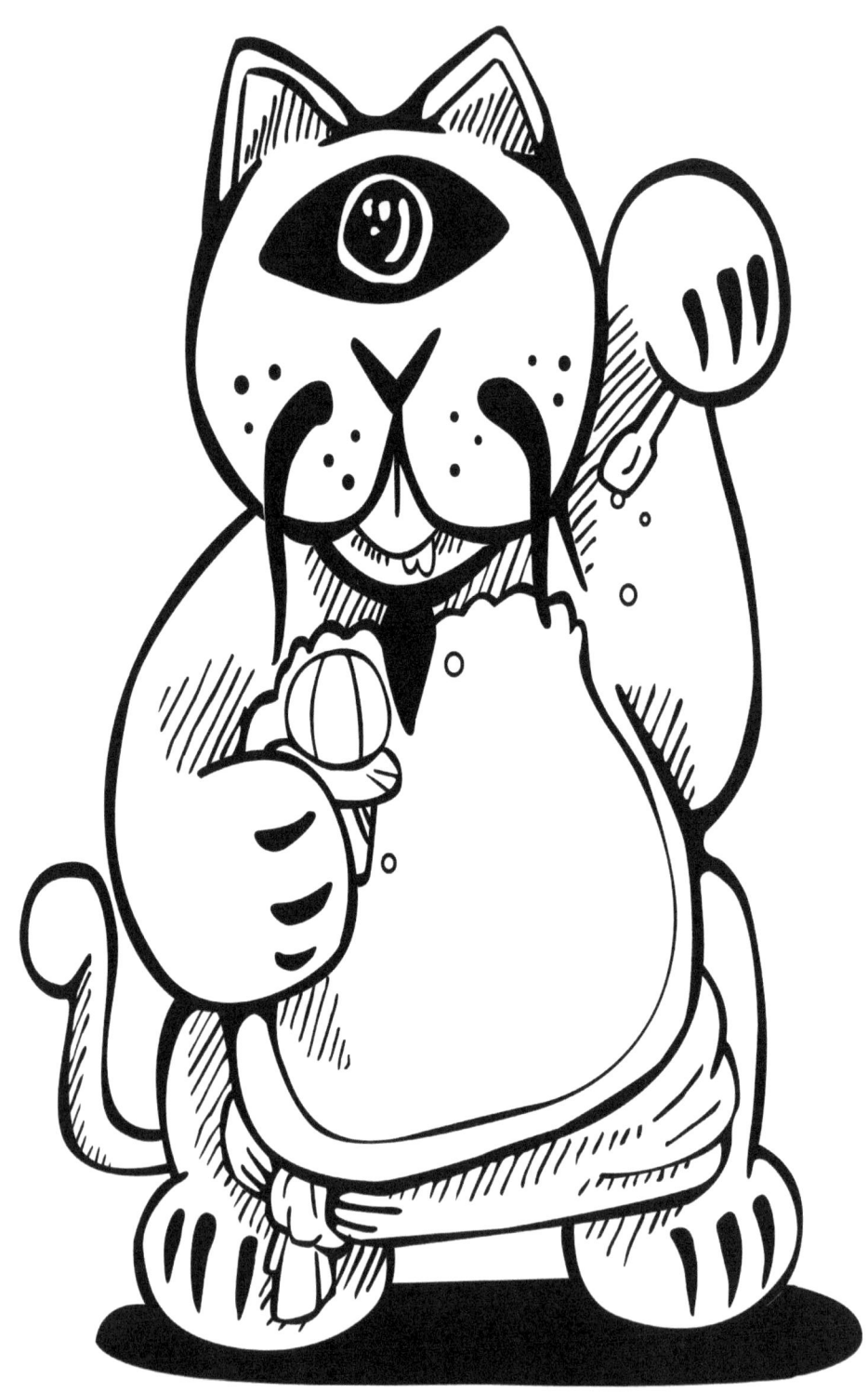

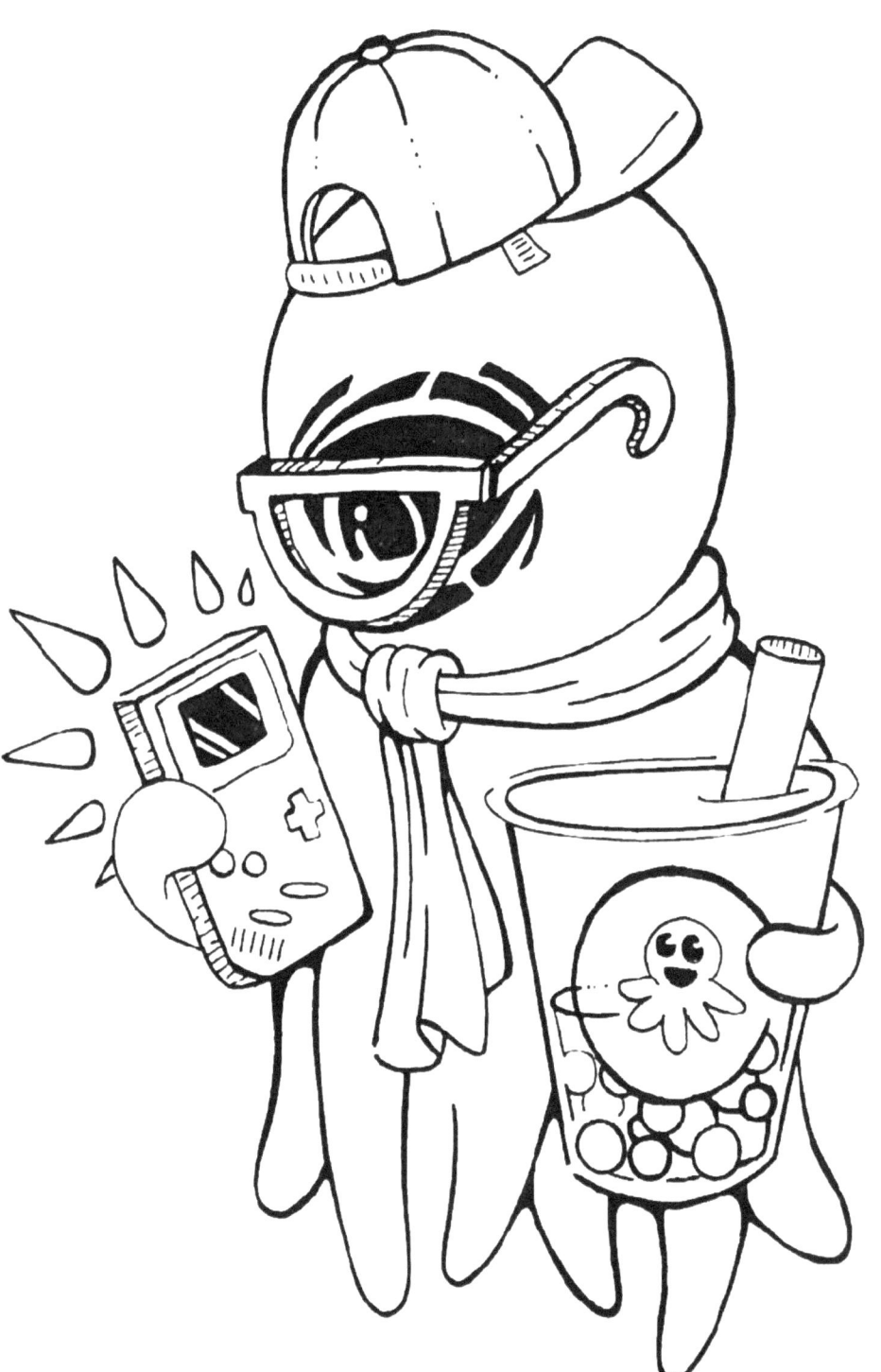

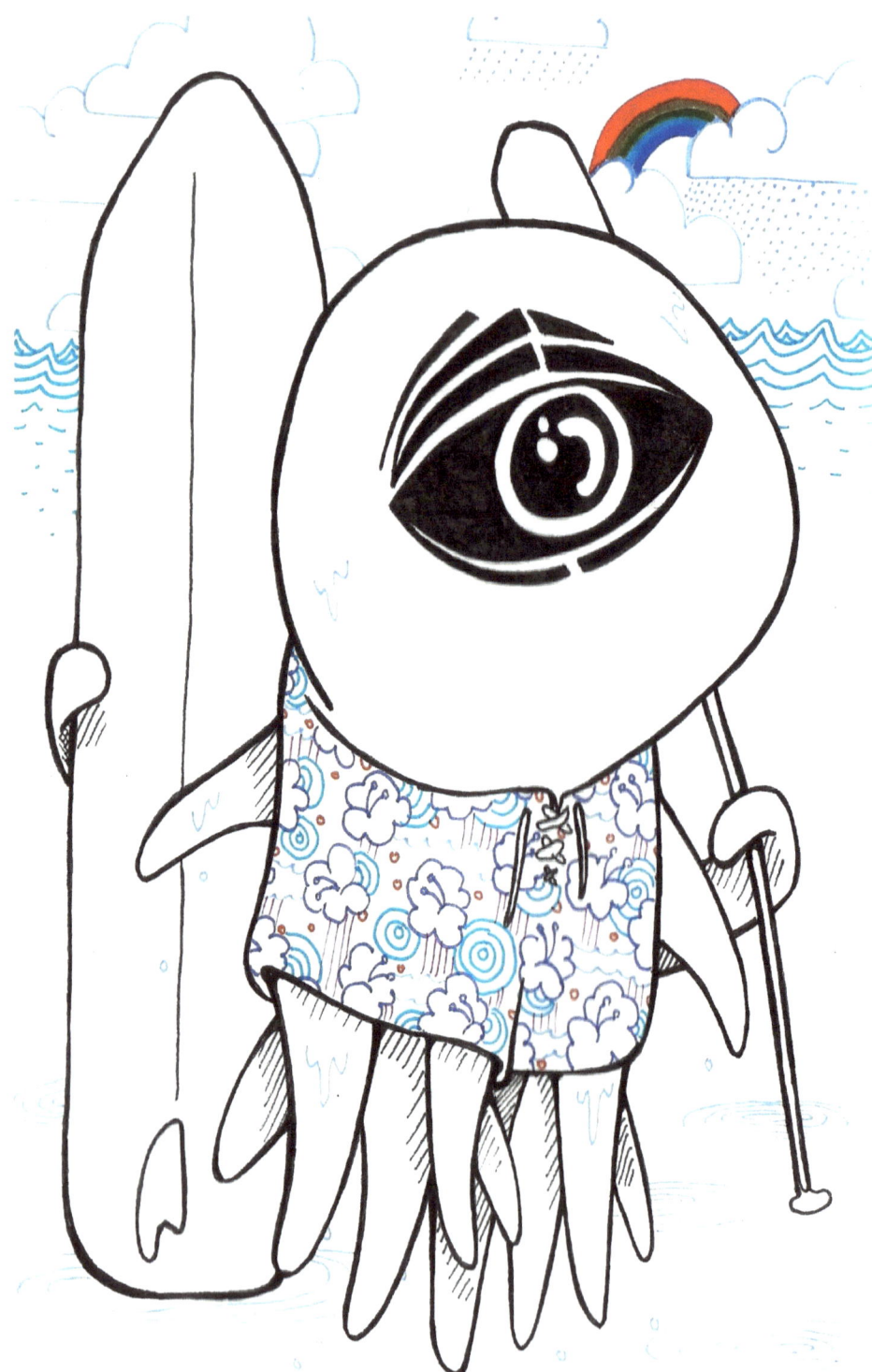

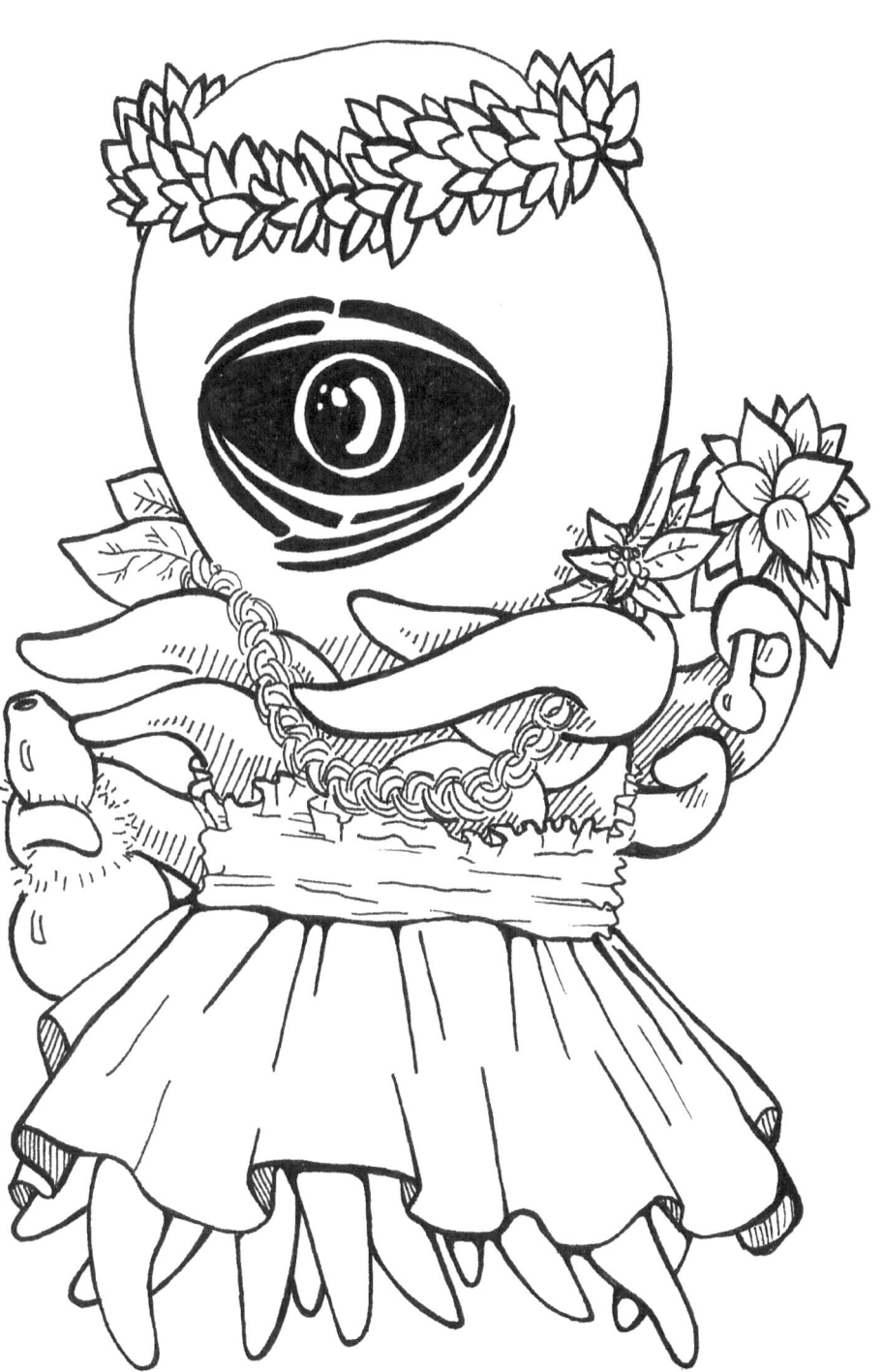

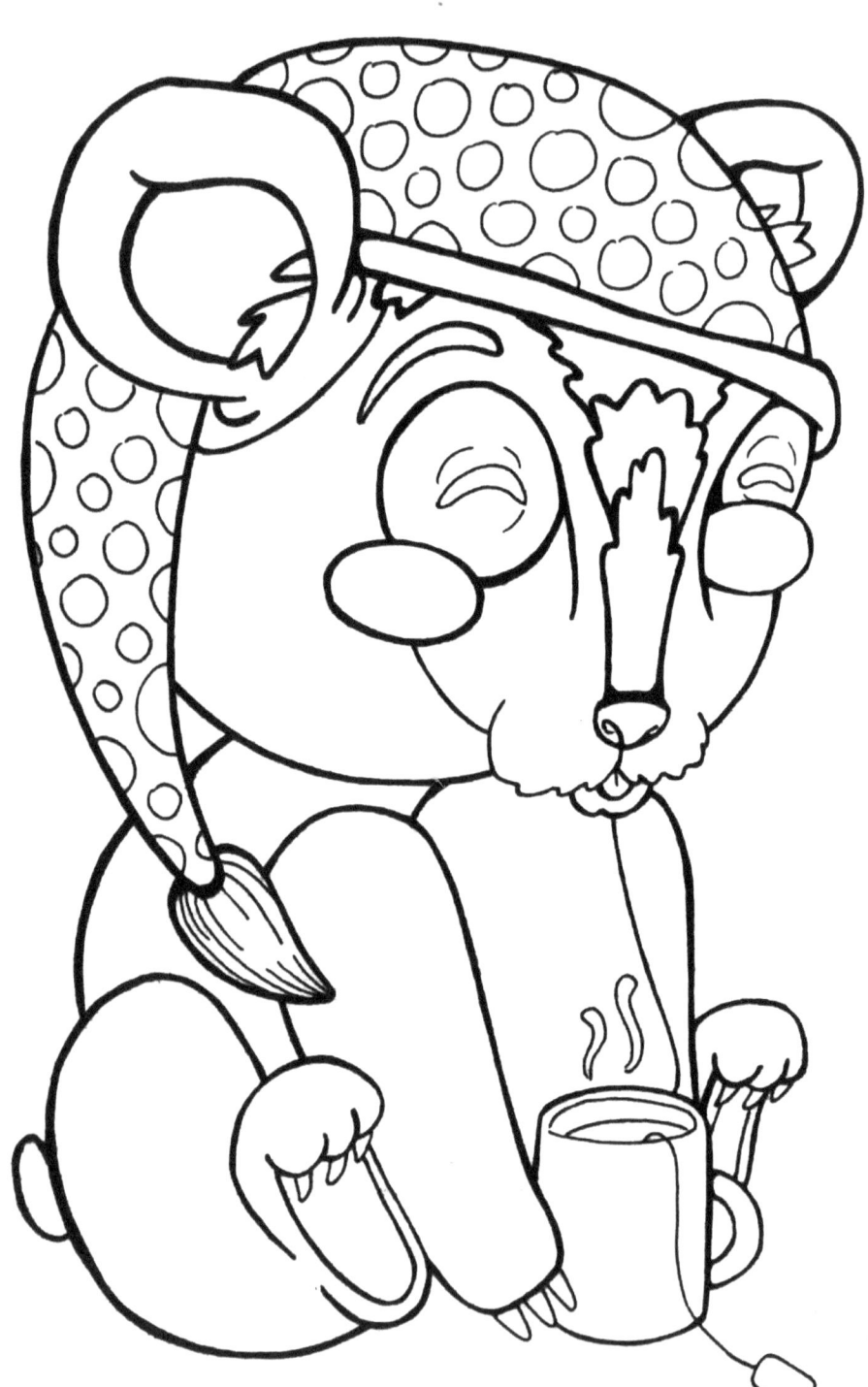

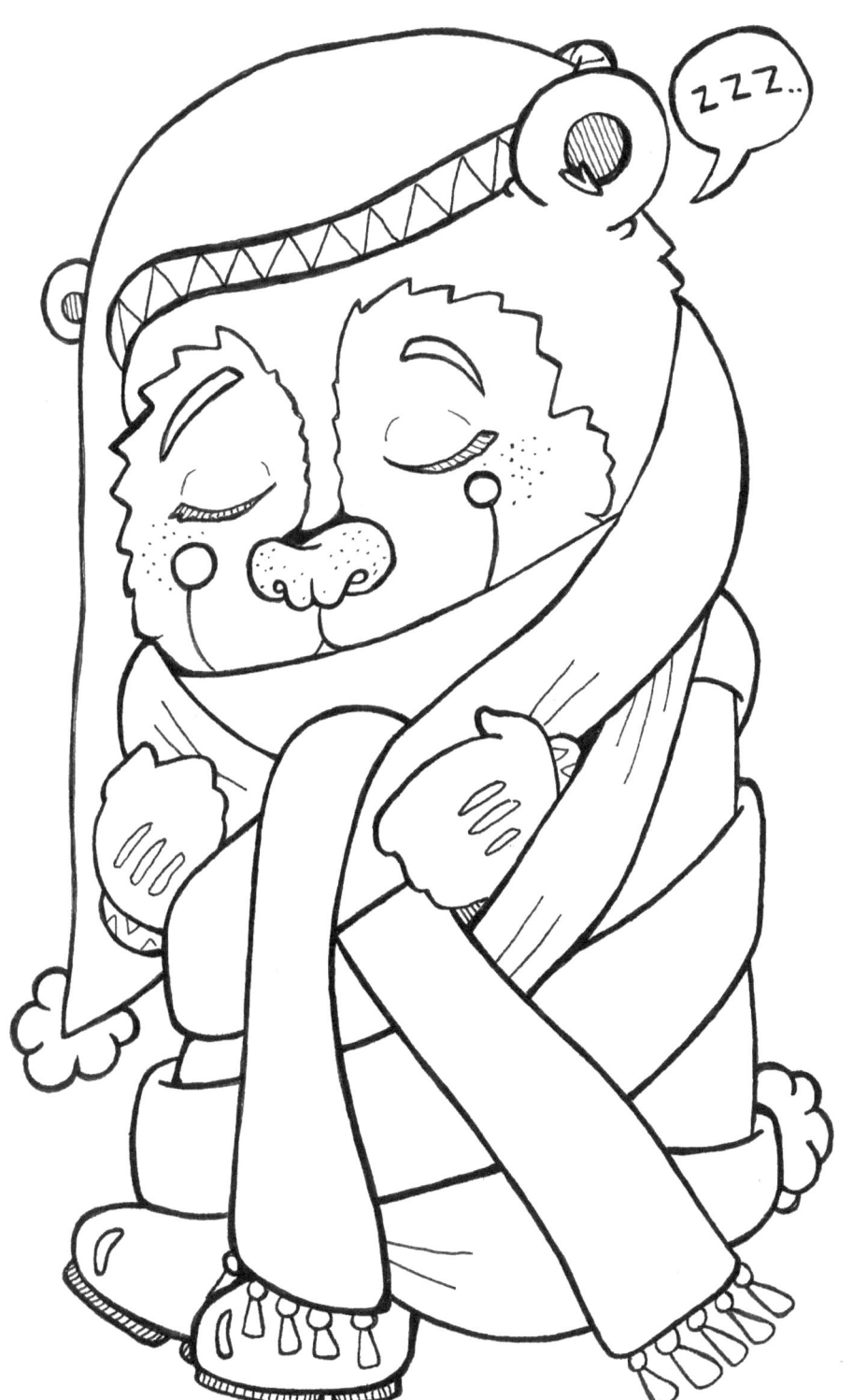

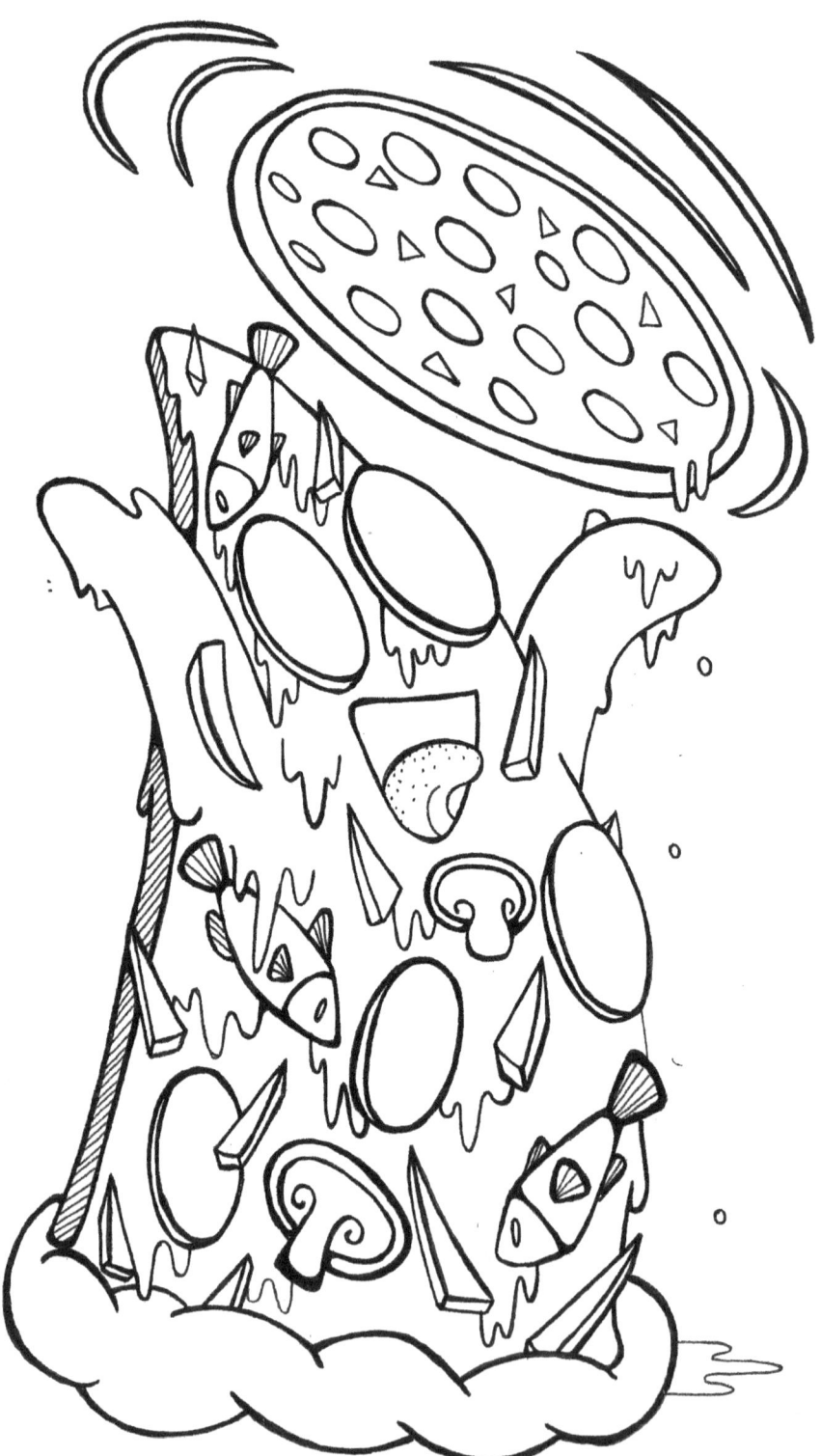

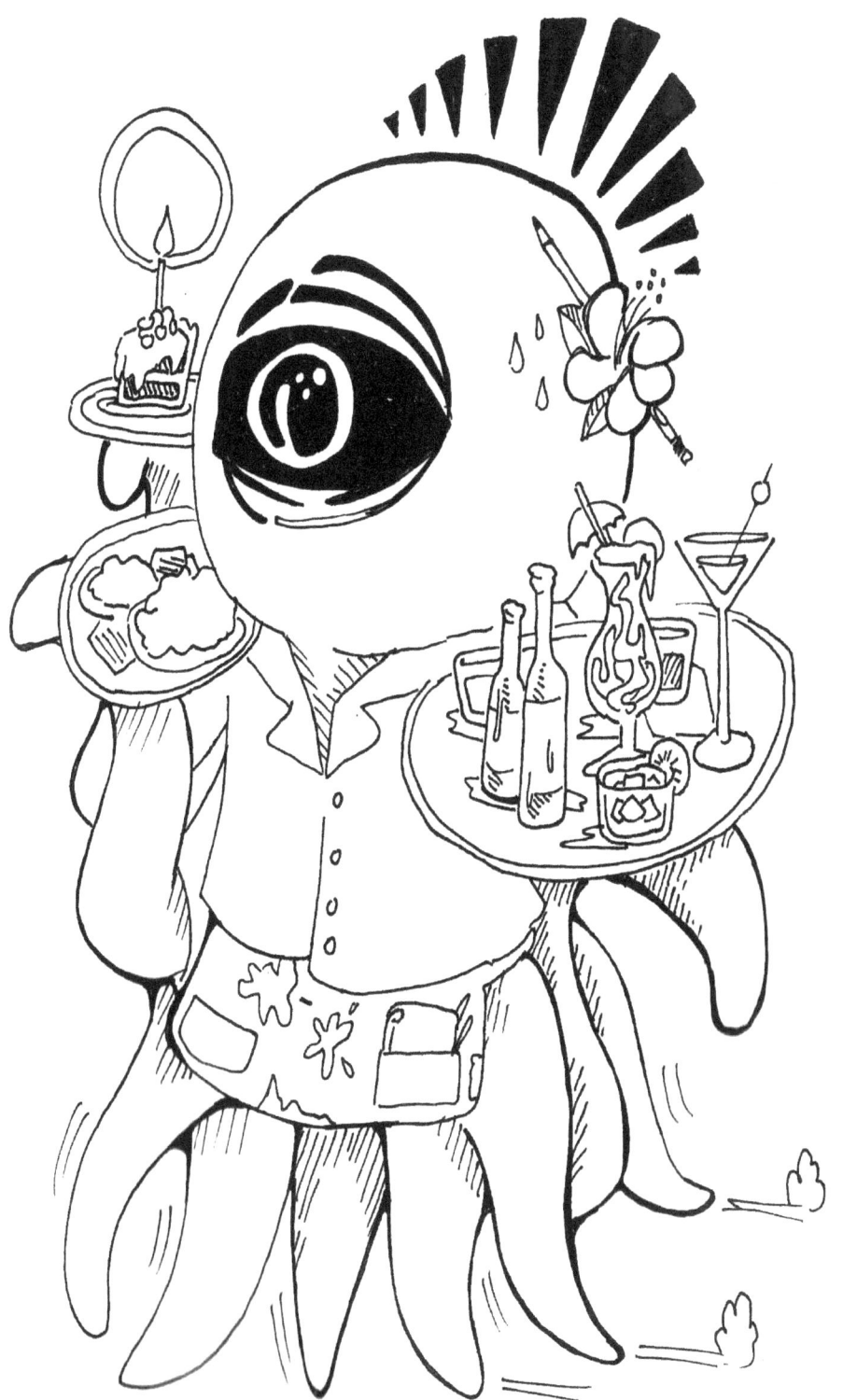

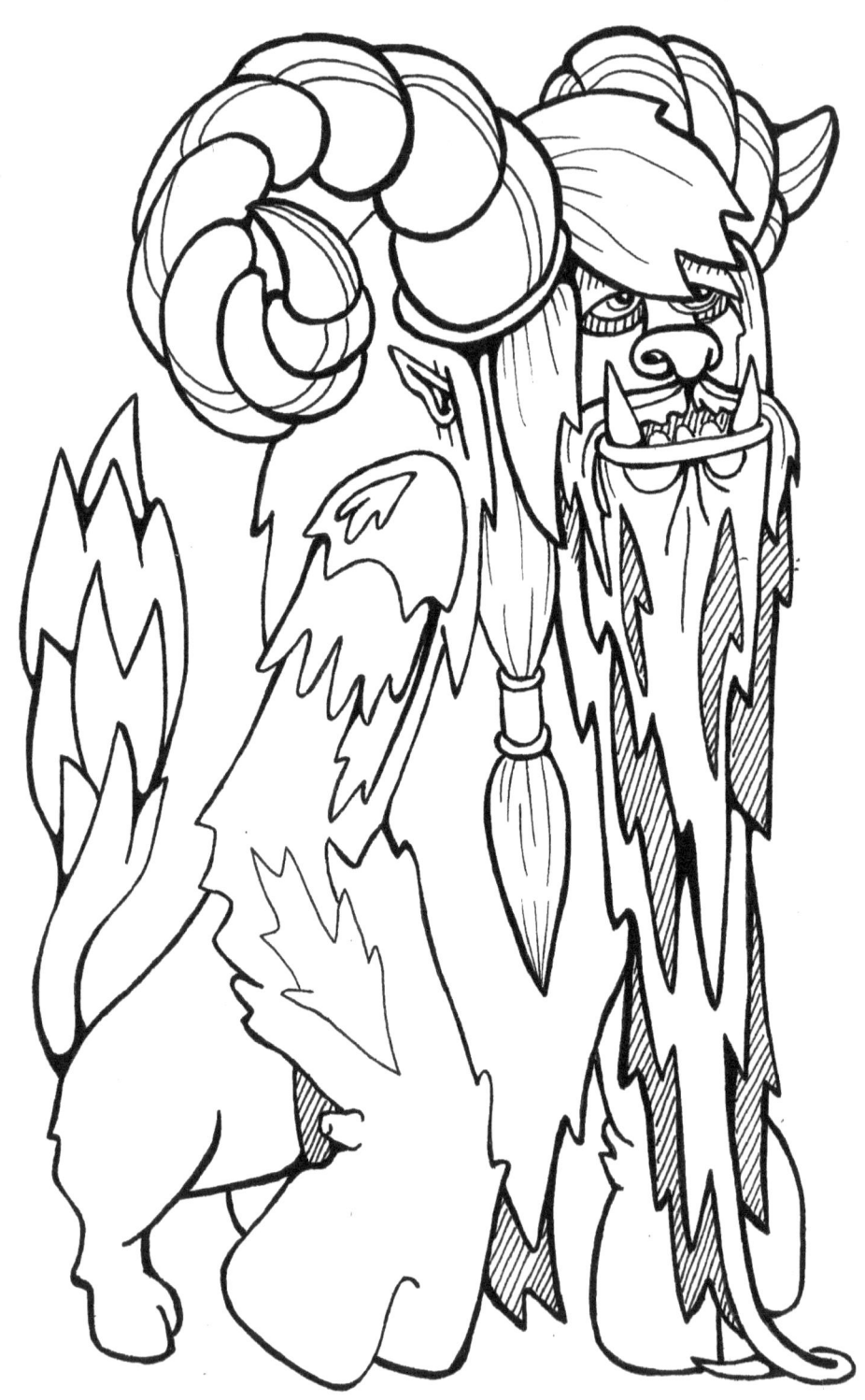

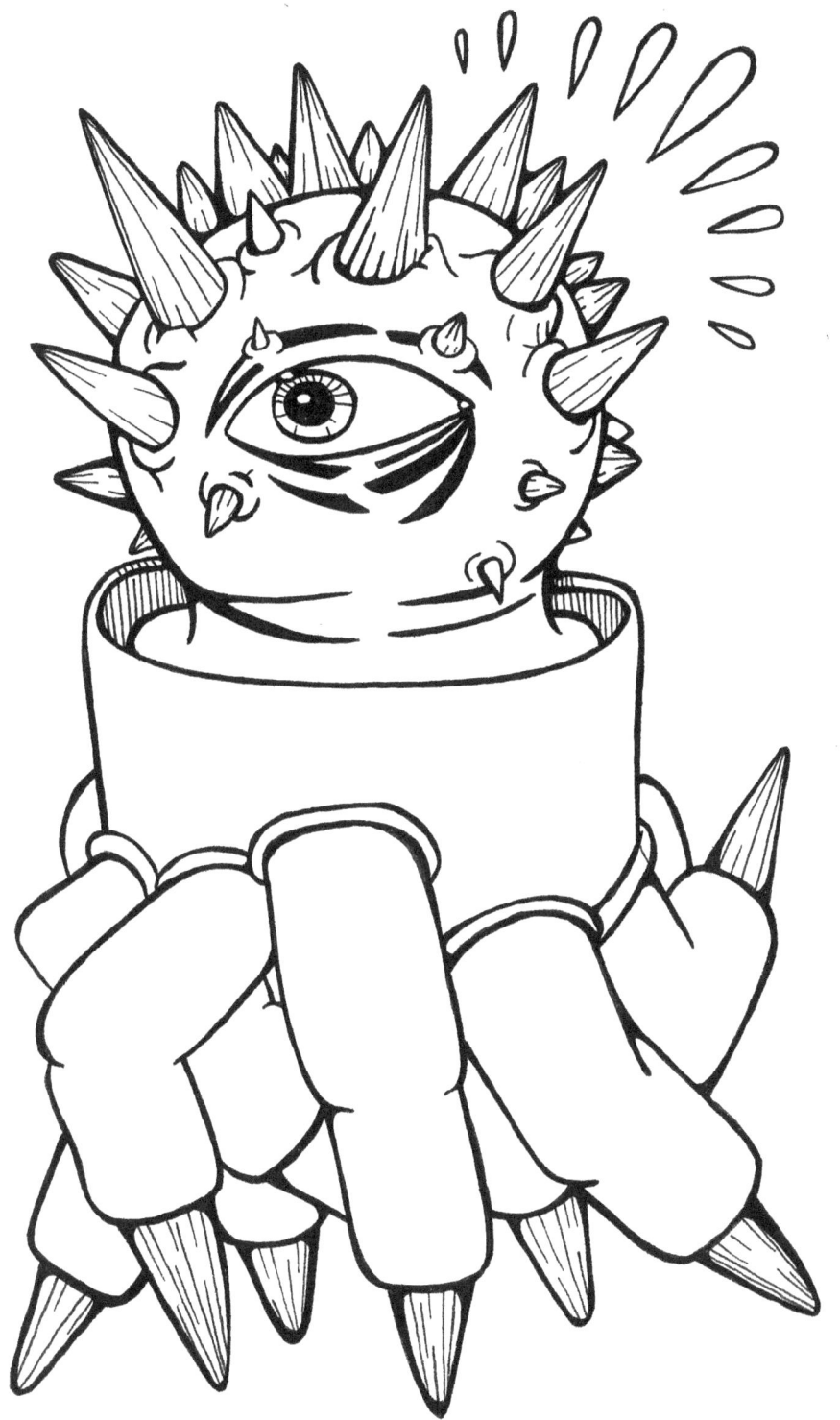

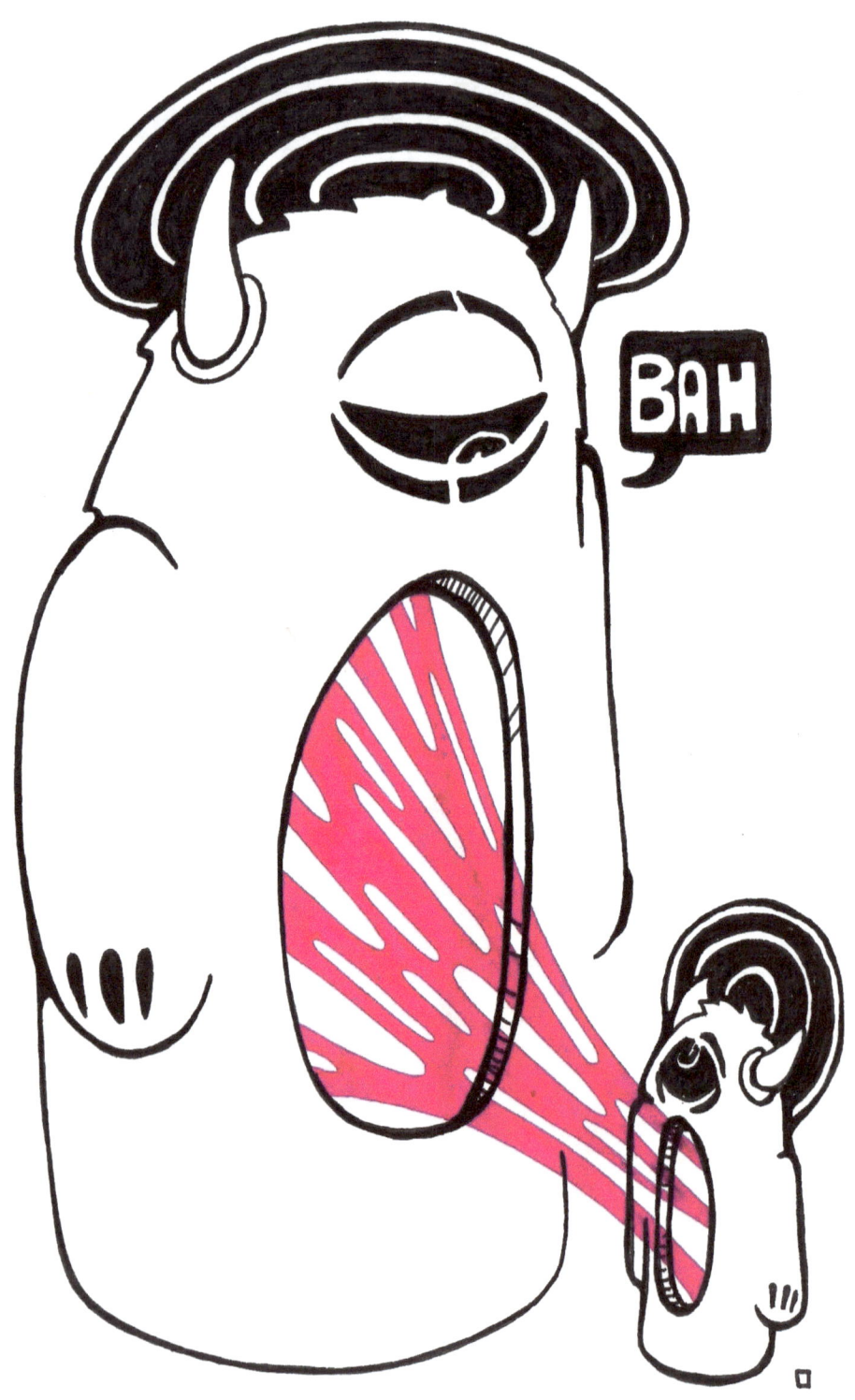

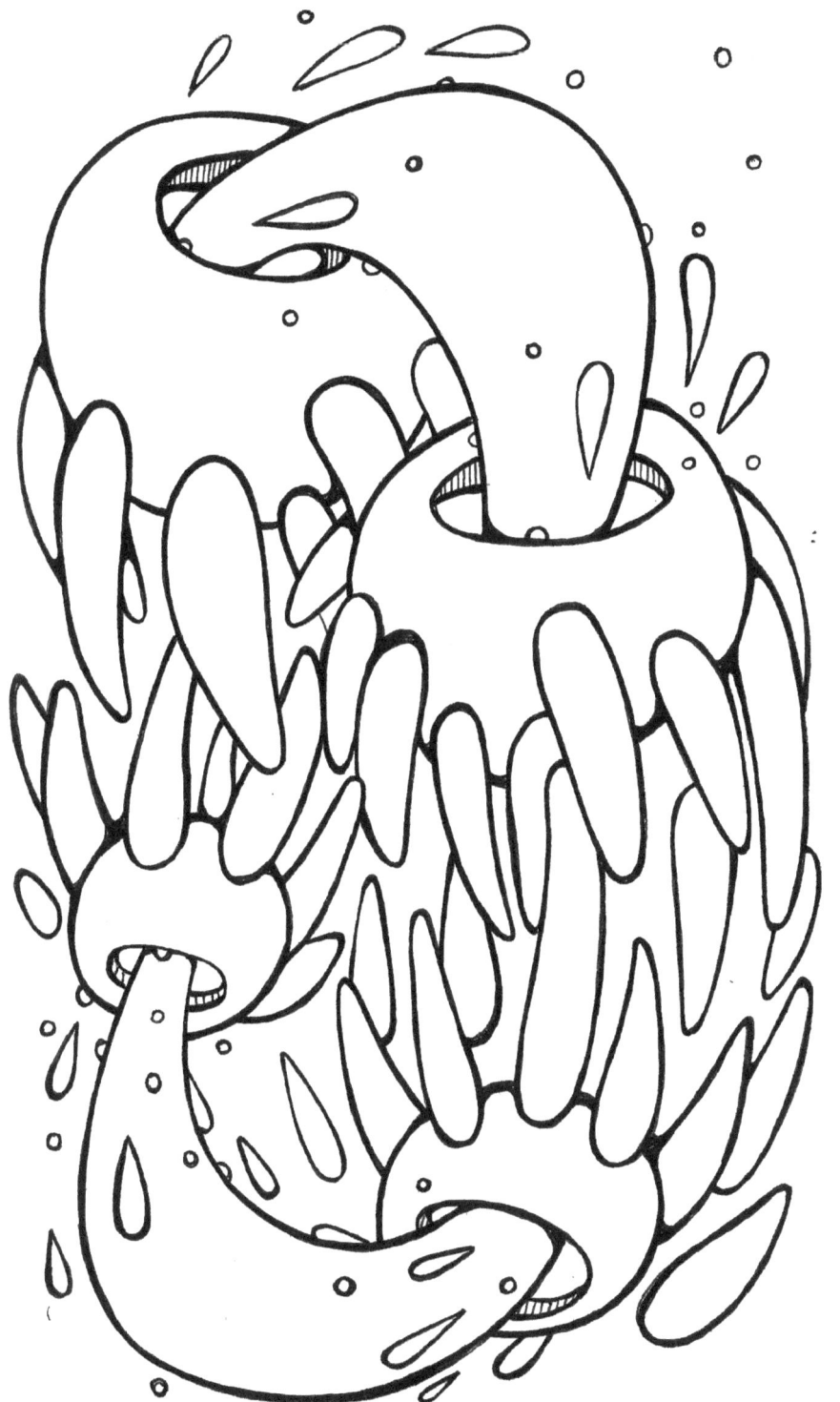

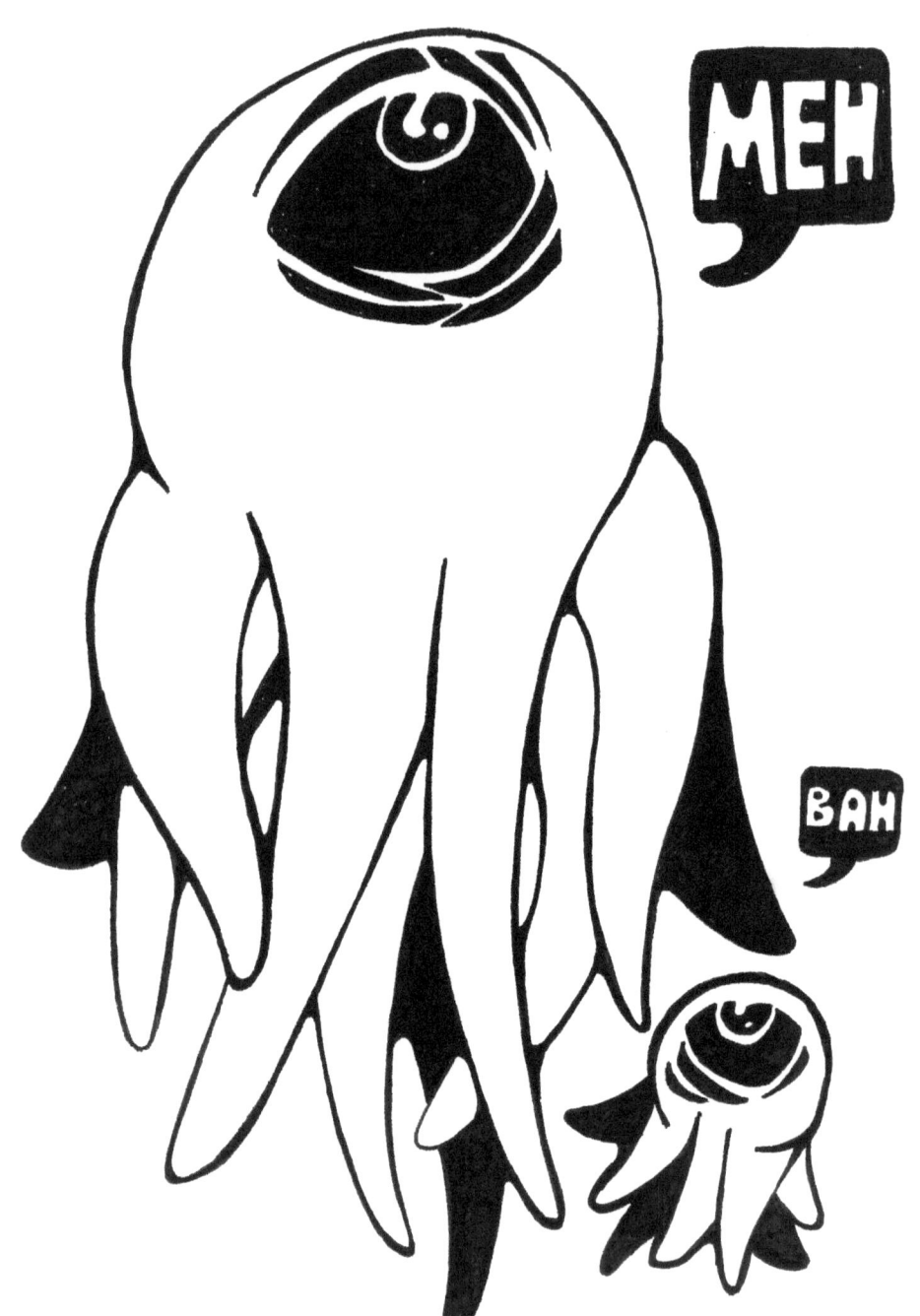

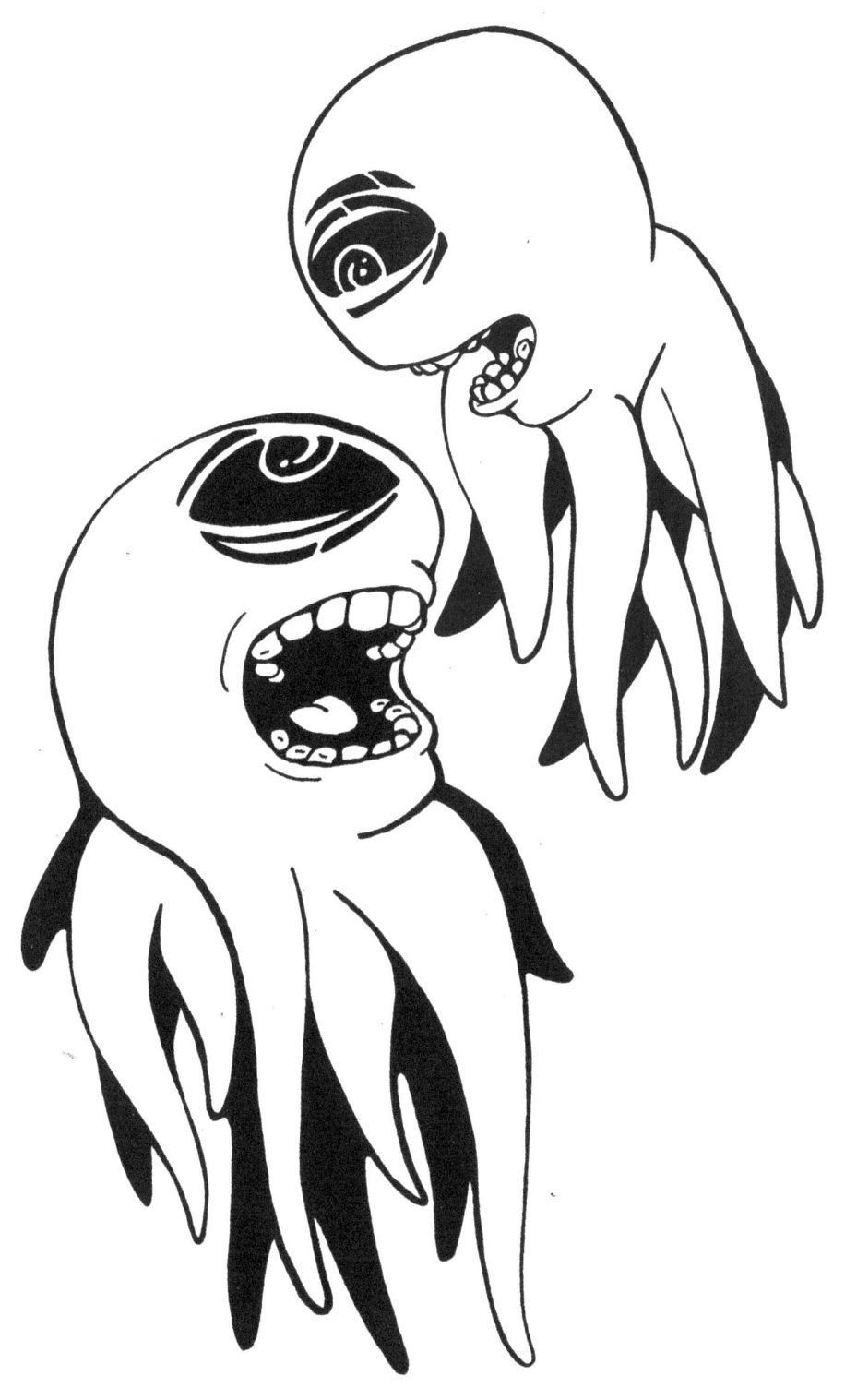

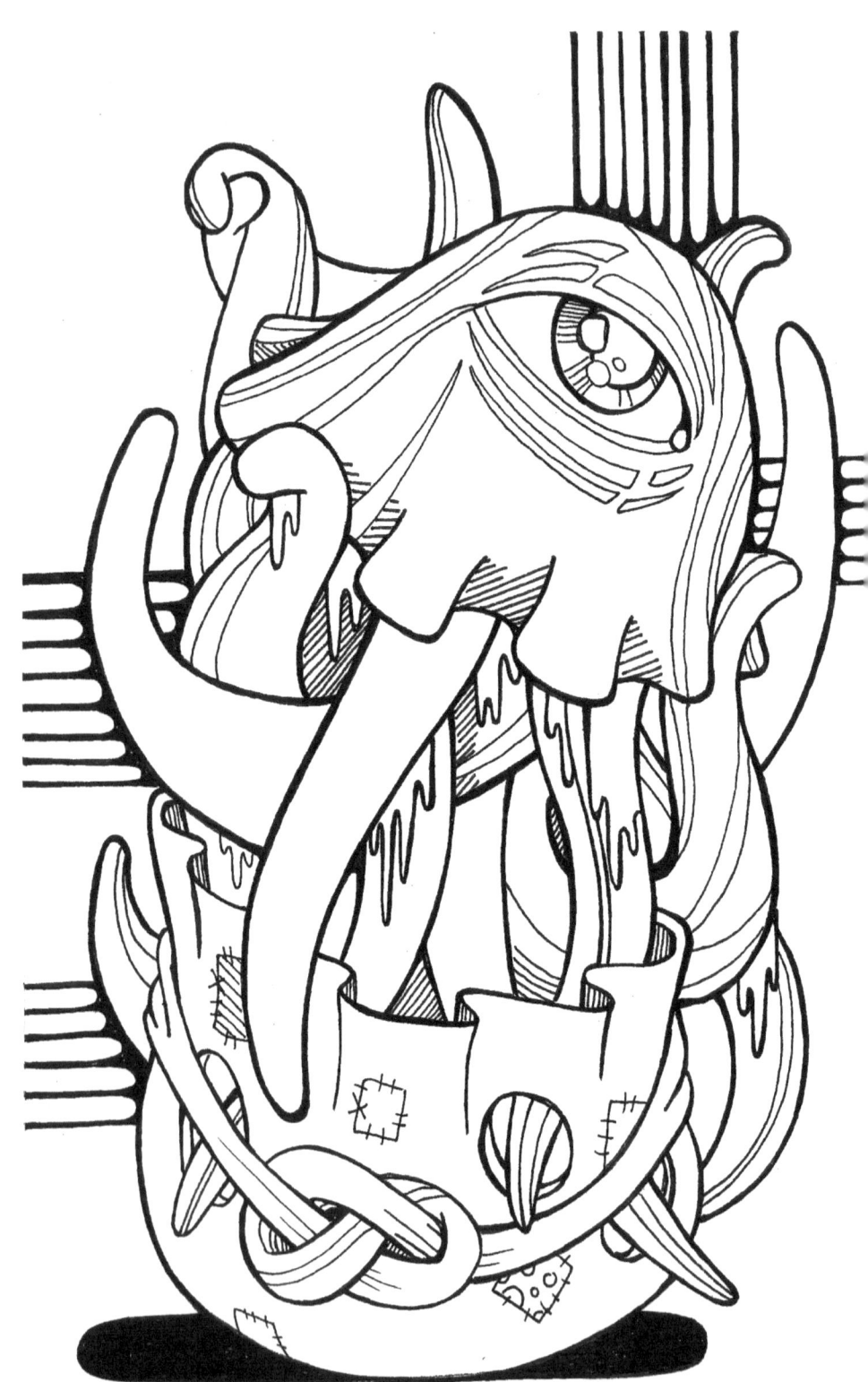